Loony
Sex Laws

Loony Sex Laws

That You Never Knew You
Were Breaking

**Robert Wayne Pelton,
author of *Loony Laws***

WALKER AND COMPANY ❋ NEW YORK

First published in the United States of America in 1992
by Walker Publishing Company, Inc.

Published simultaneously in Canada by Thomas Allen & Son
Canada, Limited, Markham, Ontario

Library of Congress Cataloging-in-Publication Data
Pelton, Robert W., 1934–
Loony sex laws : that you never knew you were breaking /
Robert Wayne Pelton.
p.   cm.
Includes index.
ISBN 0-8027-7383-4
1. Sex and law—Humor.   I. Title.
K5194.P45   1992
340'.11—dc20   92-2881
CIP

Book design by Georg Brewer

Printed in the United States of America

4   6   8   10   9   7   5   3

DEDICATED
TO
S. C. YUTER,
WHO ONCE SAID, WITH NO HUMOR INTENDED:
"LAW IS THE BACKBONE WHICH
KEEPS MAN ERECT."

Contents

CONTENTS

Part II
Loony Sex Laws Through History

Part III
Loony Sexual Court Rulings and Decisions

Preface

Women not allowed to marry eunuchs? All adulterers to be branded? No chili sauce allowed on any kind of food, for sexual reasons? Illegal for friends to masturbate together? Against the law to make love to your wife if she's still a virgin?

The noted lexicographer Samuel Johnson once remarked, "The law is the last result of human wisdom acting upon human experience for the benefit of the public." Do you agree with this bit of philosophical speculation? Let's take a sojourn into the land of laughable sexual legalese before responding to this question. Then decide!

The name sometimes fits the game. Massage parlors have been outlawed in one seemingly appropriate North Carolina community. Where? Try *Hornytown!* Nor are such massage parlors allowed in any of these communities: Lovelock, Nevada; Cumming, Georgia;

Easyville, Indiana; Peterstown, West Virginia; Loving Junction, New Mexico; Headland, Alabama; Peterborough, New Hampshire; Virgin, Utah; Loveland, Colorado; Playland, Florida; Morehead, Kentucky; Romeoville, Illinois; Loving, Texas; and Cherryland, California.

A man who decides to lasso his girlfriend in order to seduce her had better think twice about doing so in Hogansville, Georgia: An old ordinance there prohibits a male from using a lariat to subdue his prospective lover. On the other hand, nothing in this loony legislation says a woman can't lasso her man.

Elvis, Jerry Lee, or Little Richard banned in a progressive European city? Maybe! The Office for Public Order in Munich, Germany, issued a decree making it illegal for young women wearing bikinis to play rock 'n' roll music while wrestling in a pool of mud. The official logic behind this drastic legislation was said to be "for reasons of personal hygiene and because of the inherent risk of sexual orgies." By the same token, then, an identical mud-wrestling party must be fine if Dolly, Willie, and Loretta are on hand to provide background music of a more country nature.

Section 63–18 of the Municipal Code in New Orleans prohibits "an entertainer wearing the clothing of the opposite sex mingling with the public attending any place of entertainment." This law is apparently nothing more than a bad Mardi Gras joke! Been to the French Quarter and Bourbon Street lately?

Margate City, New Jersey, regulates exactly how a male surfer may or may not dress while on his surfboard in the water. No man is allowed to surf while in the nude or with a sock pulled over his privates.

Sexually active teenage girls won't have any legal problems in Hawaii, but their parents certainly will! Sections 768–11, 17, and 22 of the Revised Statutes clearly state, "Parents or guardians of an unmarried girl under eighteen years of age may be sentenced to three years of hard labor for aiding, abetting or knowingly allowing the girl to engage in coitus." Sexual activities other than coitus are apparently not outlawed for a young woman under eighteen years of age, as the law makes no mention of any. And nothing in this law specifically applies to a young man who has sex while under the age of eighteen.

In Mississippi, "fornication" is a violation of the law *only* when it takes place between a male teacher and a female student. Sexual relations between a female teacher and a male student apparently are not illegal since they're not mentioned in this odd piece of legislation.

And in good old Missouri, citizens can have private romantic interludes as often as they want. Only people caught having them in public are punished.

In eighteenth-century Italy, women were barred from marrying castrated men. But the women weren't punished for this misdeed—the eunuchs were. If caught, they were promptly flogged and then executed!

The community of Lewiston, New York, came up with a real lulu of a law! It banned the showing of any X-rated films within the town limits. Interestingly enough, at the time there were no movie theaters in Lewiston.

Buckhorn, Kentucky, is a tough place for a fellow who would enjoy taking his girlfriend or wife out for a relaxing stroll in the woods. No man is ever allowed to do this if "his sole purpose is to seduce the woman." Such activity can bring a day in the local jailhouse and a $10 fine.

Henry Ward Beecher said it all when he summed up his views on the art of lawmaking: "We bury men when they are dead, but we try to embalm the dead body of laws, keeping the corpse in sight long after the vitality has gone. It usually takes a hundred years to make a law; and then, after the law has done its work, it usually takes a hundred years to get rid of it."

Beecher has a good point! His opinion still holds true in today's fast-paced space age. Many of the old sex-related laws from all over the world are still on the books. They were once passed by supposedly intelligent legislators—but even this appears doubtful in many cases. Most, obviously based on the prejudices of the lawmakers, are biased. Many are humorous, yet rather frightening. Some are downright strange. Let's take a trip around the world, and through history, and take a close look at some of this looniness.

LOONY SEX LAWS AROUND THE WORLD

Loony Sex Laws in the United States

Be extremely careful if you're a skating instructor and decide to relocate to Indiana or Ohio. Both of these enlightened states have odd laws that prohibit male skating instructors from having sexual relations with their female students. This atrocious misdeed, called "the seduction of female students" in the ludicrous legislation, is prosecuted as a felony! This particular statute apparently applies *only* to male teachers. It seems that female skating instructors may have sex with male students.

Authorities in Harrisburg, Pennsylvania, passed a special piece of loony legislation governing sexual activities in the toll-collection booths on the Pennsylvania Turnpike. The law, which pertains only to female toll collectors, prohibits them from engaging in sex with a truck driver in the confines of a booth. Any woman violating this law will be fired for "behavior unbecoming an employee." (If for any reason the transgressor is later reinstated, she won't be allowed back pay.)

Liquor and sex always seem to go together, even in the writing of laws. Maryland prohibits the selling of condoms through vending machines in gas stations and stores—with one major exception. Prophylactics may be dispensed by a vending machine only "in places where alcoholic beverages are sold for consumption on the premises."

Vending-machine condom sales, on the other hand, are banned in such states as Hawaii, Kentucky, Massachusetts, Pennsylvania and Wisconsin. Yes, you may purchase a pack of gum, a candy bar, some potato chips, or a soft drink from a vending machine—but, alas, absolutely no condoms!

And in Texas, no one other than a "registered pharmacist" may sell condoms or other kinds of contraceptives "on the streets or other public places." No, not even physicians! Anyone who tries to make a few extra bucks doing this will be severely prosecuted for the dire act of "unlawfully practicing medicine."

No one may purchase a package of condoms at a corner drugstore anywhere in Nebraska. Only physicians can sell them while practicing medicine. In

Arkansas, condoms can be sold only by physicians and other medical practitioners. Delaware allows the sale of condoms only by doctors and wholesale druggists.

Kentucky and Idaho limit condom sales to medical practitioners and licensed pharmacists, but their license to sell the items may not be hung on a wall where it can be seen by customers. Maine, on the other hand, licenses condom sellers, and the license must always be on public display.

Nevada, with thirty-five legal bordellos, has no condom problem; the law there requires that condoms be made readily available at each brothel. The use of condoms in Nevada brothels is compulsory. No condom, no sex.

Willowdale, Oregon, has a funny law regarding the use of profanity between a married couple. It's illegal for a husband to curse or swear during lovemaking. But a wife *is* allowed to whisper the identical naughty words in her hubby's ear while in the act.

If you happen to be visiting Connorsville, Wisconsin, and are in the throes of lovemaking, be mighty cautious how you celebrate when everything ends on a perfect note. You could get into some legal difficulties.

5

City fathers have banned lovers from shooting a gun when the female partner has an orgasm. (Setting off firecrackers may be safely assumed to be legal for this purpose, as the law makes no mention of anything other than a gun.)

Clinton, Oklahoma, is apparently a community with unusually high moral standards. The city fathers have banned local men from masturbating while observing a couple making love in the back seat of a parked car in a drive-in theater. Such a peeper can be fined and jailed for "molesting a vehicle."

North Carolina has a law on the books against "Peeping Toms," but the legislation is somewhat biased! It's illegal in that state for a man to peep through a window at a woman—yet it's *not* against the law for a woman to peep into a room occupied by a man. (Nor is it a violation of the law if a man peeps at another man!)

California husbands and wives can both still get a fifteen-year penitentiary term for engaging in certain sexual practices. They are specifically prohibited from engaging in any oral activities—even in the privacy of their own bedroom.

Try to avoid going through Skullbone, Tennessee, if you desire a little sex while driving. The law there bans a woman from "pleasuring a man" while he is sitting behind the wheel of any moving vehicle. Any man stopped and found with the front of his pants undone can be fined a minimum of $50 and serve thirty days in jail.

In Oblong, Illinois, it's strictly against the law to make love while hunting or fishing on your wedding day! No man may legally fool around with his new bride while out in the wilds on this special day.

Married, yet want to mess around a little on the side? If so, be careful where you decide to play. In California, adultery is punishable by a $1,000 fine and/or one year in prison. But adultery in Arkansas is much cheaper—offenders are fined a mere $20 to $100.

If you live in Michigan and feel an uncontrollable desire to have a fulfilling physical encounter with someone of the opposite sex, please restrain yourself! Take a trip to Texas or Virginia before succumbing to your sensual desires. Why? Because single guys and gals who are caught in the act in Michigan can be fined as much as $5,000, and they could be sentenced to as many as five years in prison. Single adults in Texas who are apprehended while having sex are charged with a misdemeanor and given a $500 fine. On the other hand, singles in Virginia who get caught spend no time in jail, and the fine is a paltry $20 to $100, according to the court's judgment.

Branchville, South Carolina, retains a wonderful old piece of loony legalese covering those who "lewdly and lasciviously associate, bed, and cohabit together, in a public or non-public place." The amorous couple can be punished with a $500 fine and as much as a six-month prison term.

Single folks have it relatively easy in Rhode Island. This state still prohibits unmarried people from partaking of bedroom activities under any circumstances. However, if caught, the lovers are both fined $10.

Unmarried adults in Arizona who decide to fool around a little are committing a serious felony! Anyone single, man or woman, caught having sex can be sent to the penitentiary for three full years.

Many variations of sexual fun and games have apparently been a popular pastime in societies throughout history. Ancient Roman art regularly depicts quite a number of these activities. So does the art of bygone Greece. Drawings by the ancient Egyptians include the same things. It's found even in paintings done by prehistoric cave dwellers. Despite such artistic license, many of the United States still punish certain bedroom antics rather severely. For example, South Dakota (Compiled Laws 22–22–21) threatens a ten-year prison term for "copulation by means of mouth." Utah (Code 76–53–22) has made this same act a misdemeanor; there, oral sex brings a six-month jail term and a $299 fine. Rhode Island (General Laws 11–10–1) labels it an "abominable, detestable crime against nature," and such activity brings a seven- to ten-year stretch in the penitentiary. It is outlawed in New Mexico (Statutes 40–A–9–6), where participation is punishable by a $5,000 fine and a two- to ten-year sentence. Florida (Statutes 800.01) chastises with a twenty-year prison sentence those who take part in this act.

Maryland still has a unique law on the books regarding what it calls "perverted" or "unnatural" sex acts. The law is one of the most explicitly worded in the nation: "Every person who shall be convicted of taking into his or her mouth the sexual organ of any other person or animal, or who shall be convicted of placing his or her sexual organ in the mouth of any other person or animal, shall be fined."

Men can still be arrested and punished for the crime of "patronizing a prostitute." This is the law in such places as New York, Kansas, Illinois, and Connecticut—which gives a "john" three years in prison. Go

9

to Kansas if you really must do business with a hooker. It's only one month in jail and a $500 fine for anyone who gets caught. Better yet, visit Nevada, where prostitution is legal. (The state actually has had within its borders an organization called the Nevada Brothel Association!)

A gentleman can be incarcerated for from one to ten years in an Arizona or Washington, D.C., prison for "causing his wife to be a prostitute." A man can also get ten years in Arkansas and twenty years in Maine and Michigan for "placing" his spouse in a brothel. And in Missouri it's a "high misdemeanor" for a fellow to "force" his wife to sell sexual services on the streets.

Don't import an Asian woman and make her a prostitute in California. If you're caught, you could get a year in prison and a $500 fine.

Buckfield, Maine, has a rather unusual law regarding cab drivers and sex. The legislation declares that no taxi driver "will be allowed" to charge a fare to any passenger who gives him "sexual favors" in return for a ride home from a nightclub or other "establishment which serves alcoholic beverages," or any "place of business" selling liquor.

10

Carlsbad, New Mexico, retains a law making it illegal under certain conditions for couples to have sex in a parked vehicle during their lunch break from work. The car or van must have tightly drawn curtains to stop strangers from peeking inside while the activity is taking place.

It's against the law in Beanville, Vermont, for a road map to be printed and sold or given away if it contains advertising of a "lewd or lascivious nature." The ban specifically includes ads for massage parlors and hot tubs, as both are believed to be of a "sensual bent."

Taking an extended vacation trip in the wilderness? Like to have a refreshing bath now and then? Well, think twice before you do when camping anywhere near Cattle Creek, Colorado. An old law there bans a man or his wife from making love while bathing "in any lake, river or stream." In other words, anyone who wants to fool around while bathing must do so in a tub, or not at all.

Incredible as this may sound, it's against the law to make love to a virgin, whatever the circumstances, anywhere in the state of Washington. According to the wording of the legislation, it's a major crime even to marry and then spend the night with a virgin bride in this enlightened area of the nation. Washington's unique legislation reads: "Every person who shall seduce and have sexual intercourse with any female of previously chaste character shall be punished by imprisonment in the state penitentiary for not more than five (5) years or in the county jail for not more than one (1) year or by a fine of $1000 or by both fine and imprisonment."

Liberty Corner, New Jersey, is a place for lovers to avoid if they enjoy making out in an automobile. If the horn accidentally sounds while a couple is having sex in the front seat of a car, it's considered to be an "obnoxious activity." Each of the participants can be fined.

Anniston, Alabama, certainly isn't paradise for a liberated woman who might enjoy making love in a pool hall. An old ordinance bans women from using promises of certain physical activities to pay off a bet on a match they are playing. Nor may they initiate sex while hanging around a pool hall.

No woman may have sex with a man while riding in an ambulance within the boundaries of quiet little Tremonton, Utah. If caught, the woman is charged with a "sexual misdemeanor," and "her name is to be published in the local newspaper." The male isn't charged with anything, nor is his name revealed.

Bozeman, Montana, has legislation that bans sexual activity between members of the opposite gender who are found nude in the front yard of a home after the sun goes down. (If doing it in the front yard while naked is outlawed, then making love while wearing socks or other items of clothing must be okay!)

Women who go out on the streets alone at night in Kansas City, Kansas, can be arrested under an obscure 1901 city ordinance. Any unattended females can be picked up by the police if they are "in the streets or any public place without lawful business and without giving a good accounting of themselves."

The law in Cottonwood, Arizona, says nothing about a couple making love in a car with a flat tire. But lawmakers there did ban people from doing this while inside an automobile with "flat wheels." If the vehicle with flat wheels is parked, and you're caught making love in the front seat, it's a $25 fine. But if you're caught playing around while in the back seat, the fine is doubled! If your offense is making love while driving such a flat-wheeled vehicle, the fine jumps to $100 for the first offense and $150 for all offenses

13

thereafter. (No one has yet been able to define "flat wheels" correctly.)

There's an odd law governing beds in all Sioux Falls, South Dakota, hotels. Every room is required to have twin beds. And these twin beds must always be a minimum of two feet apart when a couple rents a room for only *one* night. And it's illegal to make love on the floor between the beds!

Connecticut still retains an old law forbidding any kind of "private sexual behavior between consenting adults." This odd law makes absolutely no distinction between married and single couples. Is such a law an indication that Connecticut citizens should "do their thing" in public?

Would you like to try giving your lover the "cold shoulder"? An ordinance in Newcastle, Wyoming, specifically bans couples from having sex while standing inside a store's walk-in meat freezer!

The Louisiana House of Representatives believes in keeping up with the times. It hurriedly approved a unique anti-streaking law; under it, streakers can be sentenced to five years in the state penitentiary and given a $2,000 fine for streaking "while intending to arouse the desires of minors." Streaking with only the

14

"intent of arousing sexual desire" brings a violator a $100 fine and one year in prison. If it can be proven beyond doubt to the court that the streaker had "no lascivious intent," no fine or jail term is imposed.

Buggery in Nebraska (Revised Statutes 28–919) is never to be treated lightly! So-called buggery, or anal copulation, can bring a whopping twenty years in the penitentiary. And buggery in Pennsylvania (Statute 4501) is deadly serious as well. It can bring transgressors a $5,000 fine and ten years at hard labor.

South Carolina's Code of Laws 16–412 includes "the abominable crime of buggery." A $500 fine and five years in prison are the punishment. Buggery in Maryland (Code Sections 553 and 554) brings a one- to ten-year prison term. Kansas (Statute 21–3505) treats buggery more lightly. Anyone in Kansas caught engaging in this activity draws a maximum sentence of six months in jail.

Indiana and Wyoming both have laws against anyone's enticing, alluring, instigating, or helping a person under twenty-one to masturbate. This activity is known in legal circles as an act of "self pollution."

Five years in prison for masturbation? Yes! Michigan law prescribes such a stringent sentence for a man who engages "in acts of gross indecency, either in public or private." This includes mutual masturbation by two men or the simple act of solitary masturbation.

New Jersey law threatens men with a three-year sentence for "mutual masturbation." The law covers "anyone who, in private, is a party to an act of lewdness or sexual indecency with another."

One more vehicle-sex law! No one may have sex while riding in the sidecar of a motorcycle in Norfolk, Virginia, where an old ordinance outlaws anyone from doing so while cruising down a city street. Such activity is considered to be a "licentious sexual act."

When traveling, if you decide to stop overnight in Hastings, Nebraska, be aware of this loony sex law: The owner of every hotel is required to provide each guest with a clean and pressed nightshirt. No male and female—even if they are married—may sleep together in the nude. Nor may any sexual activity be undertaken except while the couple is attired in one of these plain white cotton nightshirts.

Procuring or employing an Alabama girl from 10 to 18 years old for prostitution brings a relatively mild $300 to $500 fine and six months in jail. What about a little girl in Alabama under 10 years of age? Is she not protected by the law?

No man is allowed to make love to his wife with the smell of garlic, onions, or sardines on his breath within the limits of Alexandria, Minnesota. Upon the request of his wife, he must brush his teeth or stop the activity immediately.

Having sex with a corpse certainly isn't the favorite activity of most people. Yet this deed might seem quite prevalent around the country—every state has found it necessary to impose specific penalties for such action. Here are some examples:

State	Fine	Prison Term
New Hampshire	—	Up to 1 year
Connecticut	Up to $1,000	Up to 12 months
Michigan	Up to $2,500	Up to 5 years
Idaho	—	Not less than 5 years
North Dakota	—	Up to 10 years

And finally, South Dakota takes a back seat to no one when it comes to retaining interesting old laws. Prostitutes there are still prohibited from plying their trade out of a covered wagon!

2

Loony Sex Laws in Latin America and South America

It's "an excusable act of passion" in Colombia, South America, for a man to murder his wayward wife when he finds the woman in bed with her lover. If the husband "personally witnesses the corrupt sexual activity," he's allowed to shoot his unfaithful spouse. Such adultery-related homicides aren't even prosecuted.

Censorship laws in Brazil are strict. Explicit guidelines govern pornography. No newspaper, magazine, or book is allowed to discuss any aspect of homosexuality. Pictures of nude couples can't be included in any publication. No photographs even "suggesting" sexual activity are allowed. Pictures of babies being delivered are also taboo. Banned, too, are photos of women attired in bikinis or short-shorts. And no more than one bare female breast may legally be shown on any given page of a newspaper, magazine, book, or other publication.

The use of chili sauce and similar hot spices on jail and prison food is outlawed in Peru. An edict was handed down by the Interior Minister because these items were claimed to "have aphrodisiac qualities" and would "arouse sexual desires." This bureaucrat deemed chili sauce and other spices to be "not appropriate for men who are forced to live a limited life style."

Don't try to fool around while skinny-dipping anywhere near Georgetown, Guyana. Getting caught while bathing in the nude is punishable with a coat of fresh paint! The bathers are then taken to the outskirts of Georgetown and left to fend for themselves. The law is even tougher in its effort to discourage people from having sex while skinny-dipping. The lovers are first given a coat of paint; then, both parties "will be attached to an ass and taken on a tour of the village." Finally, they'll be dropped at the edge of town and told in no uncertain terms to not bother coming back.

Sodomy has long been a serious offense in Peru. A person who has engaged in it is first dragged through the streets on a rope. Hanging comes next! Finally, the corpse is burned while fully clothed. This symbolizes the sodomite's total destruction.

Cautin Province in Chile has an edict banning the hanging on the walls of *Playboy* centerfolds and other

19

sexy pinups in any home or public building. The reason according to this decree? "It's more worthwhile to admire a good landscape than a photograph of a naked woman."

In Paramaribo, Suriname, a man who rapes a single woman won't be punished—if the rape victim agrees to marry her attacker.

Featherbeds were long ago outlawed in Buenos Aires, Argentina. Why? Because "such an indulgence induces and encourages lascivious feelings."

The alpaca (a variety of llama) appears to be the most popular four-legged bedmate for many single Peruvian guys. So prevalent, apparently, is this sexual deviance that an old law still outlaws the activity. Unmarried young men are prohibited from even having a female alpaca live in their homes or apartments.

The law in Guatemala pulls no punches in dealing with single women who have been *accused* of illicit lovemaking. Supposed female "fornicators," when seen in the streets, are to be stopped, spat upon, and beaten by the citizens of the community! Single men aren't punished at all when they've been caught in the act.

It's against the law in Belize for any man to have sex with or marry his own aunt. Masked vigilantes are allowed to take the law into their own hands and severely punish the lawbreaker, who is tied to a tree and then flogged.

Passionate kissing in public places has been outlawed in Sorocaba, Brazil. The specific kind of kiss that was banned was "the cinematographic kiss, in which salivas mix to swell the sensuality."

Panama doesn't mess around when it comes to homosexuals and homosexuality. The law declares: "If any one of these males who commit this vile practice against nature with other males, he shall be degraded, and shall remain in perpetual exile." The penalty meted out for homosexual behavior is castration. The law also covers people who aren't homosexual themselves but associate with homosexuals. "Guilt by association" brings a penalty of a shaven head, one hundred lashes, and banishment.

The law in Honduras doesn't prohibit homosexuality, yet neither does it condone the practice. Sodomy, however, is strictly banned regardless of whether it's homosexual or heterosexual.

A man in Matagalpa, Nicaragua, is required by law to divorce his wife as soon as he discovers that she's

21

committed adultery. He's in serious trouble should he fail to do so; the hapless husband may then be prosecuted for his unwillingness to take the proper and necessary course of action. A wife, on the other hand, is not permitted to divorce her husband when *he's* caught in bed with another woman. Such things are simply to be expected when it comes to men, says the law.

Peru still keeps on the books an old piece of legislation that dates all the way back to 1583. Passed by the Third Provisional Council of Lima, it states, "If there is anyone among you who commits sodomy, sinning with another man, or with a boy, or with a beast . . . Let it be known that it carries the death penalty."

In Uruguay, a husband who catches his spouse in bed with another man is given an option under the current law. He has the right to kill both the wayward wife and her lover—or he can choose to slice off his wife's nose and castrate her lover!

It's a violation of the law in Valparaiso, Chile, for any man to marry a certain kind of woman—he must never take for his bride a woman who has committed adultery. Such a woman is to be condemned forever.

A married woman in La Paz, Bolivia, is not allowed to drink more than a tiny bit of wine. One who does is considered by law to be morally and sexually lax, and her husband may divorce her for one sip too many.

A married woman in Venezuela may be accused of committing adultery, but a simple unsubstantiated accusation isn't enough to merit her punishment. All the woman has to do is "swear" her innocence and she's cleared of all charges.

Masturbation is outlawed in French Guiana because of the "danger it presents to the masturbator." The law notes that such a physical act "is recognized as a common cause of insanity." Ridiculous? Well, it wasn't but a few years ago that young people in the United States were taught that masturbation would make them go blind!

El Salvador certainly isn't the best place for a married woman to have a fling. Any "married woman who lies with the male who is not her husband" can get a six-year prison term and a $30 fine. The amount of the fine is awarded to the woman's husband as his indemnity!

A husband in Honduras is guilty of adultery *only* when he has a mistress and when he "keeps her in a notorious manner."

23

A person can be arrested in San José, Costa Rica, for "keeping a common bawdy house." Or he or she may be charged with "keeping a place . . . for the practice of indecency."

A woman can legally be a prostitute in Santa Cruz, Bolivia. But it's against the law for a prostitute to solicit customers on the streets or in other public places.

Having sex with a relative is a serious infraction in Santa Ana, El Salvador. Anyone who violates this law is punished either by exile or by hanging. (The choice isn't left up to the lawbreaker.)

In Limon, Costa Rica, both parties in an adulterous relationship are in for real trouble: Each person is subject to being beaten and drowned in punishment for their deed.

The law among the Tupies of Brazil stipulates that once a woman is married, she's required to be faithful. The same standard doesn't apply to the husband. He's allowed to have as many mistresses as he can afford to keep.

Adultery isn't always a crime in Caracas, Venezuela. It depends on how long a couple has been married.

Anyone, male or female, can play around and not be prosecuted, so long as they've been married for fewer than twelve months. After one full year of marital bliss, the same sexual activities become serious criminal offenses.

Young women in Bogotá, Colombia, are not permitted to be out alone on the streets after the sun goes down. Why? Because other people might think that they are prostitutes. The law allows the police to arrest such suspects.

A widow in Paramaribo, Suriname, who plans to remarry is required by law to first make love with a man. The statute even specifies who should be her bed partner: a member of her deceased husband's immediate family.

The law in Montevideo, Uruguay, bans a man from making love to his wife during her menstrual period. Nor is he allowed even to touch her between the waist and the knees. Anyone who violates this law is fined and publicly administered 200 lashes.

Personal revenge is allowed by law in Paraguari, Paraguay, when a man catches his wife in bed with someone else. He's permitted to kill his wife's lover, and his adulterous spouse, on the spot. But the

25

wronged husband must take *immediate* action to be considered guiltless under this law—he isn't allowed to wait and do it later. On the other hand, a wife who catches her mate in bed with a lover is not entitled to any of these privileges.

The law in Durango, Mexico, governs when a couple may have sex after the woman's period begins. Five days must be allowed from the start of the menstrual flow. Seven more days must pass for "purification." A husband must not touch his wife in any manner with his hands. Then, after these twelve days have passed, the woman must bathe. Only then can the couple make love. Anyone caught violating this old law could receive the death penalty!

A bride in Ecuador had better be prepared for her wedding night. According to the law, the girl can be returned to her parents if her new husband determines that she is not a virgin.

When a bride is deflowered in Cali, Colombia, the law says, it must be done by the husband while making love. And this initial lovemaking must take place while the bride's mother sits close by and witnesses the activity.

Promiscuity isn't illegal in Valencia, Venezuela, so long as it's kept within certain specified boundaries.

The single man or woman, says the law, shouldn't ever have sex with anyone who's deformed or who is known to be an "idiot."

Single women in Costa Rica are banned from all forms of sex. Activities specifically prohibited by the law include prostitution, fornication, and "any kind of lewd activities or behavior" with a man.

A law found in Santa Cruz, Bolivia, won't allow a man of any age to engage in sex with certain relatives and other people. Specific taboo relatives include the man's mother and his mother's sister. Nor may he have a sexual relationship with an unrelated woman and her daughter at the same time.

3

Loony Sex Laws in the Middle East

The Ayatollah Ruhollah Khomeini was apparently a man much obsessed with unique sexual legislation—especially the more loony kind. He dreamed up quite a number of oddball laws with which he could further subjugate his fellow Iranians. According to one of the great Ayatollah's decrees, lovemaking during times of fasting was illegal in Iran. His edict read: "Coitus invalidates the fast, even if the penis has penetrated the vagina only as far as the circumcision scar, and even if ejaculation does not occur. If the penis does not penetrate up to the circumcision scar, and no ejaculation takes place, the fast is valid. If a man cannot determine with certainty to what length his penis has penetrated the vagina, even if he has gone past the circumcision scar, the fast is nonetheless valid."

Lawmakers in Jordan have legislated what they consider to be the most desirable amount of sexual activity between married couples. A husband, they order, is to make love "with the wife at least once every four months."

In Abu Dhabi, United Arab Emirates, the police can arrest a person for "committing an action that would be harmful to the general public." This might be the official charge for something as harmless as kissing a woman on her cheek in a public place. The penalty is ten days in jail for both the kisser and the kissee. The "action" could even be adultery! And adultery in Abu Dhabi is punishable by death. It's all according to who makes the arrest and what the arresting officer happens to write down at the time.

Conviction of adultery in an Islamic court depends entirely on the testimony of four male witnesses or eight female witnesses. Or an accused woman can condemn herself. All she must do is stand and admit three times that she actually committed the criminal act!

King Ibn Saud's Saudi Arabia treats adulterers with firmness. Both of the guilty parties are quickly picked up by the authorities. They are securely tied in a cloth sack and stoned to death. Or the penalty for adultery might be somewhat more humane, according to the way the Saudis look at things. The guilty woman may

29

be shot in front of her illicit lover, who is then publicly beheaded.

"Sperm is always impure," decreed the Ayatollah Khomeini, "whether it comes from coitus or from involuntary emissions while asleep." Therefore, Iranians are forced by law to go through ablution—or the ritualistic washing away of impurities as in a religious rite—after being involved in certain kinds of sexual activities. (Ablution isn't necessary, however, if the sperm stays inside the woman's vagina after lovemaking is completed.)

According to Iranian law, a man is required to perform his ablutions if he ejaculates while having sexual relations with an animal.

Citizens of most Middle Eastern countries are forbidden to eat lamb under certain circumstances covered by Islamic law. The law reads, "After having sexual relations with a lamb, it is a mortal sin to eat its flesh."

In Oman, if a man has sex with a camel, a cow, or a ewe, the law says that the animal's milk becomes impure and is no longer suitable for human consumption. Oman law requires that the animal must immediately be killed and then burned! The person who sodomized the beast is required to pay its owner the dead animal's full market value.

In Lebanon, only men are legally allowed to have sex with animals. But the gender of the animal is important—it must *always* be female. A man's having sexual relations with a male animal is considered a mortal sin and brings a death penalty for those who get caught.

Also according to Lebanese law, public wrath requires that a woman be executed for fornicating with any animal—wild or domesticated!

And to end this treatise on animals and sex, the law in Iran actually suggests that sex play by their male population "with wild animals is not recommended, especially with a lioness." What is recommended instead is coitus with domesticated animals such as dogs, cats, donkeys, lambs and, yes, of all things—*pigeons!*

Sodomy is also commonplace in parts of the Middle East. Again, special legislation can be found in Iran to cover this form of sexual activity. The law declares that if a man's penis fully penetrates another man's anus, ablution is also a necessity, but this time for both parties to the sex act!

31

Kuwait covers all the bases when it comes to sexual feelings. It's illegal there for a married man to glance at another woman "in a sensual manner." Nor can any male, married or single, lustfully look at a statue of a female or at a female animal!

And in Syria, a man is forbidden to "look at the body of a woman who is not his wife under any circumstances. It is also forbidden for a woman to look at the body of a man who is not her husband. It is forbidden to look at the genitals of others, even in the mirror or in a pool's reflection."

According to Iranian law, Islamic religious laws "must be obeyed and carried out by all—without exception and without argument. There is no other right, no other duty but obedience." This Middle Eastern country's Retribution Bill details the punishments for sex-related crimes such as fornication, homosexual activity, prostitution, and being a pimp. Each of these is punishable by death. Public morality is strictly enforced. Any man or woman even accused of adultery is shot.

Prostitution is a serious criminal offense in Yemen. How are transgressors punished? They are simply rounded up and publicly beheaded! (This is a lot different from the United States, where prostitutes form political organizations, appear on television talk shows, and write books about their experiences!)

No type of contraceptive may be brought into Saudi Arabia under any circumstances. The passage of legislation banning contraceptives quickly followed a World Moslem League ruling that "birth control was invented by the enemies of Islam." Anyone caught smuggling condoms, other contraceptive devices, or birth-control pills into the country is punished with a term of six months in prison.

Any and all forms of preventing conception are strictly prohibited by law throughout Qatar: "The kingdom needs more and more males for work, and more and more females to bear and raise babies."

Even physicians are thoroughly covered by Middle Eastern law when it comes to checking a woman's pubic area. Lawmakers in Bahrain have decreed that a male doctor can legally examine a woman's genitals. But any examination must be done indirectly. Says the law, "If a doctor must touch a woman's genitalia for medical reasons, he must not look directly at her genitals. He may do this only by seeing their reflection in a mirror."

"If a man remembers he is supposed to be fasting during coitus," says an Iranian law, "he must interrupt coitus immediately. If a man masturbates and ejaculates during his fasting period, his fast is invalid. If a man ejaculates involuntarily, his fast is valid; but if he does anything to [help] his involuntary ejaculation, his fast is null and void."

In Iraq, death by stoning is decreed for any married man or woman who commits adultery if marital sex is readily available. Yet, Iraqi legislators really have hearts. They proclaimed that the stones shouldn't be too big lest they kill the adulterers too quickly!

Boys and girls, according to the law in Saudi Arabia, should never be alone together unless they are brother and sister. Therefore, to prevent lovemaking before marriage, or the causes leading to this activity, boys and girls must always attend separate schools. No male of any age is *ever* permitted to enter a girls' school. Violation of the law results in public beheading of the lawbreaker.

A married man in Iran can legally have a homosexual dalliance with "the son, brother or father of his wife." His spouse can say or do nothing about this male-to-male sex. If an Iranian man "sodomizes the son, the brother or the father of his wife after marriage, the marriage is nonetheless valid."

34

Egypt has an unusual piece of loony legislation that prohibits a woman from belly dancing unless her navel is covered with gauze. Technically, according to this law, a female in Egypt may dance in public while wearing absolutely nothing more than a piece of gauze on her belly button.

Colonel Muammar el-Qaddafi's Libya has a scale of prices to be paid for prospective wives by eligible single men. They must be willing to pay the equivalent of as much as $35,000, a handful of gold coins, one healthy camel, and a number of sheep. All of these things go to the bride-to-be's father. Many Libyan males who can't afford these prices travel to Egypt and Tunisia, where a wife can be had for around $200.

The law in Doha, Qatar, even covers a naked Muslim woman who is surprised by a man while bathing or dressing. The woman is commanded first to cover her face, not her body.

In King Ibn Saud's Saudi Arabia, rapists are held in jail until Friday of each week (Friday in Saudi Arabia is the Sabbath). They are then taken from the jail and dragged to the town square. Each rapist is unceremoniously beheaded right after the midday prayers are concluded.

35

Women in Iraq are required to bathe immediately after a session of lovemaking. However, they aren't allowed to leave the room in which they made love before doing this. Their punishment for violating the law is thirty lashes.

No unmarried woman in Qatar is allowed to give birth. Such a woman is banned from using any hospital in the region. Nor can she receive any kind of medical assistance. A pregnant female who happens to be single must either flee the country or do the best she can by going it alone.

A rigorous code of Muslim sexual behavior was passed down by Iran's Ayatollah Khomeini. His followers in Iran and throughout the Middle East uphold these as holy laws to be applied sternly. They are to be obeyed and are *not* subject to change. Here are a number of Khomeini's most unusual sex-related laws.

What happens when one man sodomizes another man? According to Muslim law the sister, daughter, or mother of the man who was sodomized can never marry the sodomite. This holds true even if one or both of the men hadn't reached puberty at the time the sodomy took place. However, if the receiver of the sodomy can't *prove* that the act happened, his

sister, daughter, or mother *may* marry the man in question.

What does a person who isn't able to hide his or her genitals with "anything in particular when undressed" do? The hand is a suitable covering, according to the law.

Eating the meat of donkeys, horses, or mules is against the law if the animal when alive was sodomized by a Muslim man. If this transpired, the animal must immediately "be taken outside the city and sold."

A man who perspires when he ejaculates doesn't have to worry according to Muslim law. His sweat isn't impure, but he's not allowed to pray so long as his clothing or body are still sweaty.

What must a Muslim man do who makes love to his wife when he should be abstaining? The fellow is required to avoid praying so long as he feels or looks as if he is still sweating from the illicit activity.

What transpires when a Muslim husband becomes aroused by another woman and then makes love to his own wife? It's illegal for him to pray if he has sweated during this particular lovemaking session. But if he first made love to his wife and then made love to

37

the other woman, he can legally pray even though he may still be perspiring.

A married Muslim man who has an orgasm as a result of prolonged coitus with another woman and then has another orgasm while making love to his wife has a serious problem! He's prohibited from praying while still sweating.

A Muslim male is prohibited from staring with lust at the naked body of another man or a boy. Neither is a Muslim woman allowed to "look upon the body of another woman with lustful intent."

The law clearly states that a Muslim man can't marry a woman who was breast-fed as a baby by his grand-mother or his mother.

If a Muslim man marries a woman and makes love to her, he can't ever marry any girl his wife has breast-fed.

Muslims are banned from looking at the genitals of a corpse. The person undertaking the cleansing ritual commits a serious violation of the law if he or she sneaks a peek. The sex organs of a dead person must always be covered with a brick or a piece of wood during the ritual.

A Muslim man who makes love to his aunt isn't allowed to marry her daughters, his first cousins. But a man who marries his first cousin and then commits adultery with her mother can't get an annulment.

A Muslim man who gets married and then makes love to his wife is somewhat restrained insofar as his future sex life. He is strictly prohibited from making love to his wife's daughter or granddaughter, even if they are hers by a previous marriage.

Muslim males are also banned from marrying their own mother, sister, stepmother, or mother-in-law. Nor may they make love to their wife's paternal or maternal grandmothers or her great-grandmothers.

When a Muslim woman begins to menstruate while having sex, the man must immediately withdraw. If he can't and ejaculates instead, the fellow must, per the law, donate money to the poor. If he can't afford this, then something, however little, must be given to a beggar on the streets. Should this not be possible, the man then must, as a last resort, beg for God's forgiveness.

Marriage contracts commonly guarantee a wife's virginity in the Middle East. If the woman turns out not

39

to be a virgin as promised, the husband may have their marriage annulled.

A Muslim husband is in serious trouble if he's incapable of making love to his wife. Under these circumstances, she's allowed by law to have the marriage annulled, and the husband is required to pay her damages (one-half of the dowry as spelled out in the marriage contract).

A married Muslim woman who is caught committing adultery must be sternly repudiated by her husband. After the husband finally divorces the unfaithful woman, however, he must pay her the full amount of her dowry.

No Muslim wife may refuse or even ignore her husband's sexual advances. Any woman who does is to be judged guilty and can't get food, clothing, and a place to live from him. Nor can such a woman ask her husband to have sex with her in the future. However, should they divorce, he must pay her damages that constitute part or all of her dowry.

4

Loony Sex Laws Throughout Asia

In recent decades, China has indoctrinated its citizens to ignore their sexual interests. Transgressors are severely chastised. Is prostitution punished? Yes! And with heavy penalties. Nevertheless, officially speaking, there are no laws against prostitution anywhere in Red China. Why? Because, according to a member of the Communist Chinese Foreign Ministry in Beijing, "There is no prostitution in China. However, we do have some women who make love for money."

Bestiality laws in Bangkok, Thailand? There are none. Any man who "forcibly subdues and has sexual intercourse" with a female dog is merely charged with "cruelty to animals." The culprit is fined a small amount of money. If the female dog happens to be in heat, the fine is slightly higher.

Hotel regulations in Ho Chi Minh City (formerly Saigon), Vietnam, are direct and to the point. Al-

though the existence of prostitution isn't acknowledged by the government, there is an interesting law:
"Any visitor occupying a room must fill in a police
form. If any other person makes use of the room, she
must also register, whatever the length of her stay."

West Bengal in India bans kisses in movies made or
seen there. Why do the authorities so severely prohibit film smooches? Because, according to the Minister of Education, they "might cause great harm to
society, as they would act as a brain softener."

Any person caught circulating pornographic pictures
in Shanghai and many other parts of Communist
China is given an automatic death sentence. The guilty
party, unlike in the United States and other Western
nations, is executed soon thereafter. But determining
a person's guilt or innocence isn't the job of a Chinese
court. An attorney from the People's Republic of
China puts it this way: "Under the Chinese system,
you're guilty until you admit to your guilt and then
you're doubly guilty."

Japan has numerous laws on the books designed to
remove explicit sex scenes from adult movies. But
because sounds were overlooked by the people who
initially wrote the legislation, a brand-new law was
added. This requires a Code of Ethics Commission to

snip out all "independent groans" a person would hear while watching an adult movie.

A Kurni male in Bengal is allowed by law to have as many wives and lovers as he wants. A wife can be thrown out of the house any time the husband sees fit to do so. The law also requires that every married woman wear an iron ring on her arm. All the Kurni husband must do to divorce his wife is take the iron ring off her arm and put it on another woman.

Females who visit Communist China are expected to maintain a degree of modesty while staying in a hotel. Women are prohibited from walking around their hotel room in the nude. A woman may be naked only while in the bathroom.

In many parts of rural Malaysia, the law dealing with incest is simple. Anyone, male or female, who is caught having sex with a relative is immediately punished. The guilty parties are first bound and then buried alive next to their already-deceased family members. Everyone in the village is required to help carry out the penalty.

No one in Nepal, Bangladesh, or Macao will ever see scenes in movies of simulated lovemaking, the pubic area of a man or a woman, or even one bared breast.

Nor does the strict law even allow kisses to be shown in any film that includes actors who are citizens of these three countries.

The law in India says that special maids can be kept in a home to do more than just dusting and the laundry. Such young and attractive women are called *phashta-phashti*. They do the usual household chores. And they're expected to also take care of the sexual needs of any unmarried young men in the household.

In Utar Pradish, one of India's states, a law requires that any man who is known to have fathered three children must be sterilized. The government gives a man a transistor radio as a "good conduct prize" if he willingly submits to the sterilization. If a male fails to comply with this legislation, he can be sentenced to a two-year prison term. And he would be castrated while serving his time! The villagers in some parts of India are afraid to be seen in public or even to sleep in their own homes. Why? Because they might be found and picked up by roving "official sterilization teams." Rural areas with the highest number of sterilizations each year are rewarded with badly needed irrigation and drinking-water facilities.

Indonesian men who masturbate will never do so again. The law is extremely rough on them. They're decapitated on the spot!

44

In southern India, an old law requires that a nine-yard-long sari be draped around a woman's body and over her shoulder. The woman's breasts are to be left bare. This law has a historic origin: Mongol conquerors in the Middle Ages had decreed that any women entering a ruler's palace had to uncover her breasts, in order to show she wasn't a man coming disguised as a woman in order to assassinate the ruler.

The law in Bhutan doesn't allow a younger brother to lose his virginity before an older brother loses his. Nor may a younger brother marry before an older brother marries.

Laotians have always looked upon a woman's feet as the most erotic part of her body. Many years ago, a law was passed commanding women not to allow their toes to be seen in public. The legislation condemned "the mischievous device of sandals that evokes temptations." A Laotian husband was even given the right to punish his wife by forbidding her to wear shoes for a specified number of days. Such discipline kept the woman in a virtual jail because she knew that it was indecent to go out in public with her bare feet exposed.

A sterile husband in Singapore is allowed by law to have a child by proxy. Naturally, the more attractive

45

his wife, the easier it is to get someone else to attempt to impregnate her. The law in Singapore reads: "Where there are no children, the progeny desired may be obtained through the union of the bride, duly authorized, with a brother or other relative. The seed and what comes from it belong of right to the owner of the field." In other words, any offspring resulting from this activity is legally to be credited to the sterile spouse.

In the rural areas of Cambodia, a man has the legal right to kill the seducer of his wife, if the man had sex with her in the husband's home. If the seducer had instead had sex with the wife outside the home, the offended husband is instead allowed to put his unfaithful wife to death.

In India's Oddar tribe, a woman is allowed to live with, and make love with, only one husband at a time. But Oddar law allows women to have eighteen different husbands during her lifetime.

Japanese bachelors and wayward husbands can play around all they wish. But they're *never* allowed to do so with a married woman or with a "respectable" single female. Such activity is considered a heinous crime and warrants at the very least a stiff prison term.

46

Rural women in India's state of Rajasthan are required by law to eat carrot seeds as a contraceptive.

Taiwan's Defense Minister handed down a decree banning women in the military from wearing high-heeled shoes. Why such an odd law? Because, says the edict, "Soldiers in high heels appear more suited for love than war."

A man in rural China may allow other men to gaze upon his wife's naked body—with one exception. It's illegal for him to let anyone, other than himself, look upon her naked feet. He has the right, as well as the obligation, to kill any man who does.

There are men living in the rural areas of Guam who have a most interesting job. These fellows simply travel around the countryside and deflower young maidens before they are to be married. The girls actually pay these men to be the first to have sex with them and take their virginity. This is an absolute must, for the law doesn't allow virginal females to marry.

In Hong Kong, a betrayed woman is allowed legally to do away with her adulterous husband, but only with her bare hands. The husband's lover can also be killed in like manner by the forsaken wife.

47

Being romantic with a new-found sweetie is almost an impossibility in Beijing, China. According to the law in this country, even something as innocent as dancing cheek-to-cheek is taboo. Why? Because, the Chinese authorities claim, it "will inevitably lead to a sexual encounter." Anyone who tries to dance in this fashion will be forcibly ejected from a dance hall or ballroom.

Virginity remains at a premium in rural Taiwan. A woman who plans to marry must first appear in the nude before witnesses. These people later have to attest to the fact that the girl is untouched by men.

A widow in Burma is well covered by law, but certainly not favorably. Such a woman must stay isolated from society for one year after her husband's death. She isn't allowed to eat the flesh of a horse during this time. Indulging in any kind of sex is taboo. Should she be caught with a secret lover, the relatives of her dead spouse have the right to kill her.

In Indonesia, a suitor can make love to a girl he's engaged to and then casually drop her by the wayside. But the law comes down hard on a man who seduces or is seduced by a married woman and gets caught in bed with her. The poor fellow will get a brutal whipping followed by a long sentence in jail. But, even

48

more important, the fellow is blacklisted and will *never* be able to find a job.

Among the people in rural Malaysia, the eldest son inherits all of his father's wives, except for the one who's his mother. However, he is prohibited by law from having sex with these women—except for the special one he selects—until twelve months have passed following the death of his father.

Prostitution was legalized in Japan in 1626 and became a most popular pastime for Japanese husbands. A massive and legal red-light district was established in Tokyo. It was called the Yoshiwara, or "meadow of happiness."

Kissing on the lips is outlawed in the People's Republic of China. Why? Because, according to some faceless bureaucrat, it makes young men and women feel sensual. And it is said also to transmit the hepatitis B virus. Red China's *Workers Daily* warns readers: "We must rid ourselves of this nasty kissing habit."

Men who wish to marry a young woman among the Cols in India's Singboum district must by law first purchase her. Since marriageable females are rare in this part of the world, parents are allowed to sell their daughters. A pretty young woman can bring as much as thirty to forty head of cattle.

The penalty for single people having sex in Nepal is flogging. The sentence for a man caught repeatedly having sex with a single woman is life imprisonment. The law against adultery in Nepal is even tougher. The dunking stool is commonly used when adulterers get caught. Each of the guilty parties is securely tied to a chair mounted on a sturdy board. The chairs are slowly lowered into the water and covered. Just before drowning occurs, the chairs are raised up and out of the water. The adulterers can be heard sputtering and choking. They are once again immersed in the water. This torture continues until the accused no longer sputter and choke. They are dead!

Anyone in the People's Republic of China who wishes to marry must first obtain permission from the government. After the wedding, the newlyweds must request permission to bed down together.

Adulterers are punished in Bhutan by stoning. Should the husband or wife step in and try to save the adulterous spouse from the stoning, he or she, too, will be stoned to death.

The law in Taiwan allows for a friend or relative of the groom to perform a special service on the wedding night: He is to stand in for the groom and have sex with the new bride. His main responsibility is to "deflower" her in case the groom is unwilling or unable to handle the situation.

Chin P'ing Mei was an erotic novel enjoyed by the Chinese for centuries. Yet a 1725 law made the book illegal for anyone to read or even to possess. The law is specific regarding penalties for anyone buying the novel or for owning a copy:

Booksellers:	100-lash flogging
	Ostracism for a 3-year period.
Military personnel:	100-lash flogging
	Banishment for 3,000 leagues (3 miles)
Citizens:	100-lash flogging

Officials in government were simply "degraded." As could be expected, they got off the easiest.

5

Loony Sex Laws in the Russias and Eastern Europe

Bigamy is strictly against the law in Hungary. Any man who has more than one wife at the same time is punished in a most unusual manner: Bigamists must, by law, "live with both wives simultaneously, in the same house." What about female bigamists? They aren't even seriously considered under Hungarian law!

There'll be no lovemaking in Riga, Latvia, while a couple is fighting, verbally or otherwise. The law says that married people aren't allowed to make love while they are arguing.

Physicians throughout the former Soviet Union are permitted to give extremely limited lectures on sexual subjects to medical students. But such talks can never be given to mixed groups of males and females at the same time. The Ministry of Health has made it illegal for the physicians to discuss any form of lovemaking in the classroom. Talking about positions, orgasms,

and innumerable other things is said to "excite un-
healthy interest in the public."

Kaunas, Lithuania, has an unusual law regarding a
mother-in-law. She can be "banned from the house"
by the husband whenever he wishes to make love to
his wife. But he isn't required to give his mother-in-
law any particular reason for her banishment. The
same law doesn't give a wife the same privilege.

The Russian city of Volgrad must really be a fun place
in which to live. Lovemaking techniques are highly
restricted according to an old law. Only traditional
sexual intercourse is allowed—and it has to be in the
missionary position (the man above the woman, face
to face). Lovers must also always have the shades
carefully drawn and all lights turned out!

Rather bored with your current sex life? Well, be on
guard if you happen to be sexually active anywhere
within the borders of Tallinn, Estonia. An old law
still on the books there bans a couple from playing
chess in bed during lovemaking.

Don't expect to be treated nicely in the Russian city
of Sverdlovsk if you try to have sex on a tombstone
while strolling through a cemetery after dark. Local
lawmakers have passed an ordinance making it illegal

for couples to have sex on any tombstone within fifty feet of a path or road, or any place "open to public view."

What exactly are the laws regarding prostitution throughout the Russias? Technically, according to the authorities, there can't be any. Why? Because prostitution is said not to exist in Russia or Hungary or Romania or anywhere else in Eastern Europe. According to the government, the social conditions responsible for prostitution simply do not exist anywhere in Russia or in her former satellite nations. Yes, the Russian police *do* pick up doxies plying their trade around the Hotel Metropole in Moscow or on the streets in other cities. And, yes, the girls are hustled off to a police precinct. Once there, they are made to sweep, mop, and generally clean the place, and then they are released. Yet the police insist that they aren't picking up prostitutes!

In the former Soviet Union, women are prohibited from wearing any sort of sheer or translucent apparel—not even pantyhose and stockings—in any public place.

Homosexuality is outlawed in Albania whether it's between men or between women. Two men or two

women are never allowed to sleep in the same bed. This is true even when they aren't homosexuals.

People in Ploiesti, Romania, can't make love during the day. By government decree, only nighttime hours are allowed for lovemaking. And couples making love at night are sternly advised to turn out all the lights first, and then pull up the sheets and blankets.

Imagine how quiet it must be around construction sites in Dresden, Germany. It's against the law for a man there to whistle, stare, wink, or make off-color remarks or erotic suggestions to any woman who strolls by on the sidewalk, other than his wife.

In Prague, Czechoslovakia, unmarried and unchaperoned females may not stand around on street corners and ogle passing males. Such "loitering" women can be fined and jailed for what is called "misconduct unbecoming a woman."

St. Petersburg (formerly Leningrad) must really be a wild town as wild towns in Russia go! Local politicos, better known as "party bosses," were apparently determined to wipe out "licentious behavior in women" or what is better known as prostitution. Their statute, seemingly trying to cover every possible bit of ground, banned such things as loitering, abusive and

obscene language, promiscuity, nighttime wandering, and cohabitation.

It's perfectly legal in Byelorussia for a man to beat his wife as a prelude to lovemaking, the rationale being that men who aren't wife beaters don't really love their wives.

In Lithuania, it's illegal to drink vodka while undergoing treatment for a venereal disease. It's also illegal to refuse treatment. A person found guilty must pay all medical costs of any person he or she has infected.

When a hero and heroine kiss in a play or other dramatic production in Poland, it must always be done carefully. Such kisses, per the law, can't plant "impure" or sensual thoughts in the minds of the people in the audience.

An old ordinance in Yerevan, Armenia, regulates the way local women may dress or undress. No woman, per this law, is allowed to take off all of her clothing in a room in which a man or a boy happen to be standing or sitting. Nor may a woman stand before her husband while naked in a room with the lights on.

The word *sex* has finally been mandated by Moscow to appear in the National Encyclopedia. Spelled *cekc* in the Cyrillic alphabet, it's defined as follows: "The combination of mental reactions, experiences, intentions and actions with the expression and satisfaction of the sexual urge."

No children? This situation is also covered by law in Ploiesti, Romania. A man is allowed to discard his wife after they've been married for ten years under certain circumstances: He may divorce her if she has borne him no children.

How much lovemaking is required in a marriage? The law in Minsk, Byelorussia, says that a man may refrain from any and all bedroom activities for one full week. But he can't refrain from making love to his wife for more than two weeks at a stretch.

Under Nikita Khrushchev, a law was passed in 1962 with regard to art in what was then the Soviet Union. Khrushchev unexpectedly dropped in on an exhibition being held at a Moscow art gallery. He became incensed upon seeing numerous paintings of unclothed women in a variety of poses. From that day on, Russian art galleries were forbidden to put paintings of nude females on public display.

57

An old law in Yugoslavia makes it illegal for a cow or a bull to mate near a public road or highway. Such activity is regarded as especially offensive if the mating is done when it can be observed by women and children. But this kind of law shouldn't be much of a problem to Yugoslavians. This country actually has fewer paved roads and highways than does the tiny state of Rhode Island.

Even Peeping Toms are covered by unusual laws. For example, a man can't peep into the window of a Krasnoyarsk couple's flat and watch them as they make love. A man peeping in Cherepovets had better be fully clothed when caught by the authorities. If undressed to any extent, the fellow will be given a thorough beating and sent home.

Do you like to leave the lights on while making love? Don't expect to do this while visiting Budapest, Hungary. It's against the law to have sex in a room while any light is burning, a fire is romantically crackling in a fireplace, or even while a candle is gently flickering.

No person, male or female, is allowed to have sex with a goat, a cow, a hog, or any other kind of animal in Krakow, Poland. Getting caught in the act brings twenty lashes in a public place for a first offense. Second-time offenders are punished with one hundred

58

lashes. And a third-time offender is simply put out of his or her misery—with a single bullet to the head.

A director or an actor has been prohibited by law in the former Soviet Union from showing any degree of sensuality and passion between a man and a woman in a film or a play. Violators of the law are thoroughly blacklisted. They are banned from working on films or in the theater. Nothing about them can appear in print. And they face a jail term.

Parks in Russia are nice for strolling or relaxing while sitting on a bench. But don't try to embrace and smooch your spouse or sweetheart! Even a simple hug or kiss is a violation of the law. Such public demonstrations of affection may lead to more sexual permissiveness. The same is true if a couple embraces or kisses in a public square, on a park bench, or while standing in a darkened doorway. Couples who get caught breaking the law are picked up and carted off to the police precinct.

How about divorce in Panevezys, Lithuania? In almost every case, only a husband can seek a divorce. He can leave her if she has committed adultery or even if he suspects her of doing so. He can even divorce her for not being a decent cook, or for not doing his laundry satisfactorily. A wife may divorce her husband only if he contracts boils on his genitals.

Married men are seldom punished for adultery in Skopje, in the former country of Yugoslavia. But women are treated quite differently. A married woman caught in bed with another man is taken to the outer boundaries of the community. Her head is shaved and she is left to make her way back to town as best she can.

Some sex acts are considered to be "indecent" as well as "unnatural" in Gdansk, Poland. These sexual activities are illegal and are punished by the authorities. Mutual masturbation between two or more women can bring as much as one to two years processing caviar in a labor camp for females on Shikotan Island.

"Any carnal knowledge by means of an orifice other than the sex organs" is strictly forbidden in Latvia. This is true even if the lovemaking is between a married couple in the privacy of their bedroom. Also illegal, according to this particular piece of legislation, is any form of sex between homosexual males.

Single people in the former Soviet Union and Eastern Europe are prohibited from wasting time and energy pursuing lovemaking opportunities. Why? Because their leaders stress that the people must conserve their strength. This is done in order to better accomplish the tasks assigned to them by the state.

Under the direction of former Soviet President Leonid Brezhnev, a law was passed banning the appearance in the Soviet Union of "half-dressed women" on the screen. The law prohibits Russian movie makers from filming any actress while she's wearing a nightgown, underwear, or even a revealing swimsuit.

A rapist in Parnu, Estonia, will be placed in irons for seventeen years. And he must serve the full prison term.

An unfaithful husband in the house? If a wife in Wrokaw, Poland, discovers that her husband is cheating on her, the law gives her the right to take action. She may legally beat the other woman unmercifully, or she may beat her to death if she chooses. The only stipulation is that she use nothing more than a club to accomplish her goal (and that she leave her husband out of it).

Kissing on any public street, according to the law in Gorky in Russia, is an "immoral activity." So is fondling in public. Both must be avoided by people at all costs. Lip caresses and intimate touches are believed to be unfit sights for the eyes of children.

The same kind of law is found in many other places in Russia, including Moscow, Omsk, and Kirov. In these and other cities, such activities are called "immodest conduct." Those caught doing them will be labeled "corrupt." Their name and photograph will be placed on public notice bulletin boards all over the city. They'll also lose their apartment as well as their job and will find it impossible to get another one.

Any homosexual found guilty of male prostitution in Plovdiv, Bulgaria, is automatically found guilty of "infamous conduct." He is made a noncitizen with no rights and may receive six years at hard labor in an especially unpleasant prison work camp.

Guys and gals with a strong bent for same-sex fun and games had better be on the lookout in Russia and all of the Eastern European countries. The sexual practices of homosexual men as well as those of lesbians are considered by law to be both "aberrant" and "licentious" in such countries as Bulgaria, Yugoslavia, Hungary, and Czechoslovakia. Getting caught and then convicted of these crimes brings long and harsh sentences.

In Sofia, Bulgaria, it's taboo for a married couple to feel pleasure while making love. This is considered to be "inappropriate behavior" for the husband and wife. But erotic fun is encouraged by the same government officials when a man has an encounter with a prostitute.

6

Loony Sex Laws on the African Continent

In Johannesburg, South Africa, a woman can charge her husband a fee each time they make love. But the law specifically states that she must be careful not to "overcharge" because she might price herself out of the market. "The bed is the poor man's opera," explained one magistrate. "For a poor man, however, a charge of 10 rand a ticket might put the show beyond the realm of popular entertainment."

Newlyweds in some parts of Chad and Niger are governed by a most unusual bit of marriage legislation. The couple must retire to a mat right in the midst of their wedding celebration feast. They then initiate their first lovemaking as a married couple—in front of all their guests.

The married Apingi man of Equatorial Guinea is nicely protected by tribal law. Should he catch his wife having sex with another man, the guilty fellow becomes the husband's slave for the rest of his life.

Should his wife's lover happen to be a woman, the culprit becomes his mistress, should he desire this, for the balance of her life. Otherwise, he can sell her to someone else in the tribe.

The Wakikugu and Wakamba tribes in Mozambique have a law regarding lovemaking. Their men and women are prohibited from making love while their cattle are in the pasture. In other words, all sexual activities are banned from morning to evening.

Among certain tribes in Tanzania and Kenya, the law severely chastises adulterers. Those caught in the act are quickly punished with a death sentence.

The authorities in Kenya certainly don't fool around when it comes to streakers! Any male streaker of foreign origin will be promptly arrested. The fellow will then be escorted directly to the airport while still in the nude and put aboard the first available aircraft going to his country. Evidently, the enlightened legislation doesn't cover citizens of that African nation who might decide to streak. Nor does it cover foreign females who might decide to run around Kenya in an undressed or semi-dressed state.

Punishment for a wife's infidelity is handled on a graduated scale in Kontagora, Nigeria. A wife's left hand is chopped off when she's caught the first time while "making love with a man other than her husband." If the wife gets caught in her lover's bed a second time, she loses her right hand as well. Those foolish enough to get caught a third time are immediately decapitated! A man in Kontagora who cheats on his wife isn't charged with breaking the law.

In Zaire, adultery committed by a married woman is severely punished with an automatic death sentence. A married man, on the other hand, is free to fool around with any woman he wishes at any time during his marriage.

Among the people of Lusaka, Zambia, a married man may not commit adultery without his mate's approval. Fooling around without a spouse's permission is the only way a married person can commit adultery. And a man in Lusaka doesn't *ever* need the permission of a woman to do anything! Only a married woman can be called an adulterer by having sex with a man outside of her marriage. And a wife's sideline lovemaking is illegal only when she fails to obtain her mate's permission beforehand.

Any man who was married to Queen Zinga of the Congo was allowed by law to have as many other wives as he wanted. And he could have as many lovers as he chose to keep. But he was forbidden to have children through any of these affairs and other marriages.

The law in South Africa covers the censorship of all magazines, books, plays, movies, and "other forms of public entertainment." Everything is scrutinized by more than one hundred official censors. In South Africa, these men have the job of checking for nudity of either sex, heterosexual and homosexual sexual activities, simulated sex play, and so on. Their decision to ban a book, play, movie, or anything else is always final! It can't be appealed by taking any of the all-powerful censors to court.

The Ashanti of Ghana have a stringent law dealing with adultery. The man who has been slighted is allowed to slice off the nose of his adulterous wife.

A cuckold in Manda, Tanzania, may also cut off the nose of his unfaithful spouse. But he must first catch his wife in the act.

In Nambia, the punishment for a man who rapes a woman is up to the rapist. He has a choice between castration and serving a term of twenty years at hard labor with no chance of parole.

67

Castrating a man who rapes a woman is also legal in Zimbabwe. The rape victim is allowed to perform the castration herself if she so chooses. Castration is also the penalty for a married man who gets caught committing adultery. In this case, the man's wife can perform the deed.

Homosexuals in Liberville, Gabon, had better be on guard. Males get from seven years to life at hard labor in prison if caught fooling around with another male.

A husband in Yaounde, Cameroon, is entitled to kill his wife on the spot should he catch her in bed with another man—but he may legally do this only by slitting her throat. The wronged spouse isn't allowed to harm his wife's lover. Why? Because the woman is always held responsible when adultery occurs.

A woman in Dakar, Senegal, can do the same thing when she catches her husband fooling around. She's allowed to take her spouse's life without being punished for killing him. But she must not kill his lover. The wayward woman is to become her servant for a period of three years.

Burkina Faso and a number of other African countries aren't exactly fair when it comes to punishing wayward women. A woman can be condemned for committing adultery even though she was never caught in the act. All it takes to establish her guilt is to have three people say she was an adulteress.

Grounds for divorce in Benin can be nothing more than a wife's "perverse and disgusting sexual conduct." The husband alone decides what constitutes this. Only husbands have the right to seek a divorce.

The law in Gaborone, Botswana, determines the required frequency of lovemaking suitable for newlyweds. They are expected to make love "at least three times each month" until the bride becomes pregnant.

A husband in Lome, Togo, is the key factor in his wayward wife's punishment for committing adultery. The law states that a man has the power to pardon his wife's sexual misdeeds. He therefore decides whether she lives or is put to death!

There's a law against incest in Monrovia, Liberia. Anyone found guilty of incest is required to commit suicide or to pay an assassin to do the job for them.

Incest is also outlawed in Kankan, Guinea. The penalty is always severe and always enforced—death by public burning at the stake.

69

Kissing the "property" of another man is believed to be a telltale sign of adultery in Burundi. The law clearly spells out the punishment: "If he has kissed her—the wife of another—they shall draw his lower lip along the edge of the blade and cut it all off."

The crime of seduction as related to a single woman in Equatorial Guinea is a minor offense. Her seducer is punished with a small fine and a mild beating. But the seduction of a married woman is punished more severely—her lover is sentenced to death by drowning.

The law in Banqui, Central African Republic, is extremely harsh when it comes to pimps, procurers, and panderers. Lawmakers in this country have issued a decree that molten lead be poured down the throats of these criminal elements.

Any heterosexual or homosexual man or woman involved in sodomy in Sierra Leone will be tied to a stake and burned alive. "Sodomy" in this country, according to the law, "cannot and will not be tolerated under any circumstances."

No woman in Kampala, Uganda, is allowed to let her hands accidentally touch the genitals of any man other than her husband. Should she do so, the law requires

70

that the hand doing the touching be burned in a pot of boiling oil. A second offense calls for the "amputation of the offending hand."

In some of the more remote areas of Africa, when a husband is convicted of sodomy or incest, his entire family is punished. The husband is buried alive. His wife and children are made slaves to be used at will by all other members of the tribe.

Prostitutes in Luanda, Angola, are required by law to dress themselves so that they can be easily identified by others. They must at all times be seen with bared breasts. This, decided the authorities, would attract the attention of Luanda's young men and direct them away from homosexual liaisons.

A man in Guinea Bissau who willfully seduces another man's wife is required by law to pay a heavy fine to the wronged husband. The seducer must also cut off one of his lover's fingers or toes and eat it. After all of this, the unfaithful woman's husband is allowed to decapitate his rival should he choose to do so.

It's illegal in Gambia for any male to dress like a woman and play the part of a female. Furthermore, such a man can't work in the streets as a prostitute.

71

7

Loony Sex Laws in England and the British Isles

A law in Great Britain refers to sodomy as "the abominable crime of buggery," which, until 1861, carried the death penalty. "Buggery" now brings *some* British subjects a punishment of life in prison. Buggery is still illegal between heterosexual couples, and even behind closed doors by a husband and wife. Homosexual buggery, on the other hand, is no longer punished. It was legalized in England under the "Sexual Offenses Act" in 1967—for consenting adult males who weren't in the military or the merchant marine.

Here's one place that won't attract any men who like to wear women's clothing. An old statute in Mullingar, Ireland, prohibits any Irish citizen from "appearing in public dressed with the intent to disguise his or her sex as that of the opposite sex." A fine and jail term await men or women who violate this law.

Shakespeare is still considered the literary giant of all England. Byron, Tennyson, Chaucer, and Milton are still revered as some of Great Britain's greatest poets. But no streets can be named after any of these astoundingly talented men in one English city. The Town Council in Great Yarmouth passed an ordinance banning the naming of streets after these celebrated writers. Here's what they said: "In our opinion, the moral character of these people is not such that we should name roads after them."

A young woman in Dumbarton, Scotland, was arrested when caught having sex with two boyfriends at the same time. This *ménage à trois* earned her a charge of "lewd and lascivious conduct." This kind of sexual activity carried a $500 fine. And the young woman's name and address were published in all the local newspapers.

Authorities in Carlow, Ireland, couldn't prosecute a fellow who was caught masturbating in the front seat of his automobile. Such blatant sexual activity wasn't banned under the existing laws covering lewdness. So the masturbator was instead charged under Carlow's pornography legislation, which prohibited "displaying offensive sexual material"!

It's illegal for a man and a woman to have sex "on the steps of any church after the sun goes down" in Birmingham, England. To get caught while engaging

73

in such public lovemaking brings a charge of "disorderly conduct" and a fine of $50 for each of the
participants. Presumably it's okay to do this before
the sun goes down.

A young fellow in Northampton, England, had the
rather dubious distinction of being raped five times
by a group of five women. But, alas, he was unable to
press rape charges against his assailants! Why? Simply
because under Northampton law rape is considered to
be a crime only a male can commit.

Couples in Edinburgh, Scotland, are banned from
having sex in automobiles parked in business parking
lots or parked on public streets. Nor are they permitted to engage in lovemaking when their car is parked
on their own property—unless they are in the back
seat!

It's considered to be a "national nuisance" in Great
Britain when a man tries to solicit sex from a strange
woman in public. The man on the make can be given
a three-month jail sentence and a fine equivalent to
$180. This law wasn't passed to try and regulate
prostitution in England; rather, it was designed to
stop the average guy on the make from crudely propositioning an attractive woman immediately upon
meeting her.

74

It's illegal in Dublin, Ireland, for married couples to buy condoms or other contraceptives. And stores aren't even allowed to keep condoms on the premises. Condoms and other contraceptives can be freely imported into Ireland. But it's still against the law for anyone to advertise or sell them.

Montrose, Scotland, has an ordinance banning copulation by animals (farm stock, cats, dogs, etc.) in any public place within the city limits. The owner of any animal caught violating this law will be fined not more than £15 and/or be thrown in jail for from two to twenty-five days.

No man in Liverpool, England, is permitted to dress or undress a female mannequin in any department store while children are watching. And no children are allowed to peek up a mannequin's dress. Should this happen, the parents are held responsible and can be arrested.

No man may fondle a department-store mannequin during business hours in Glasgow, Scotland. It's also illegal for a man to "molest" a mannequin in the window of a store. Nor may a man "assault" an undressed mannequin in a storage area after a business has closed.

75

The law in Cardiff, Wales, calls it "lewd and lascivious behavior" when a single man and woman get caught having sex. The fellow is charged with "openly cohabiting and associating with a person he knows is not his spouse under circumstances that imply sexual intercourse." The guilty male is fined anywhere from £3 to £15. His lover is not prosecuted.

England still retains a number of special laws governing what can and can't be sold on Sundays. These laws are strictly enforced! According to The Shop Act of 1950, *Playboy, Penthouse,* and even most hardcore pornography can be purchased on the Sabbath. But the *Bible* cannot! Merchants who ignore this statute can be fined as much as £25.

Flashers should find Manchester, England, a wonderful place in which to live. Flashing in general is against the law, and transgressors can be prosecuted. But, for some odd reason, flashing while shopping in a supermarket or a department store *isn't* illegal! The city has no statute under which to arrest and prosecute such extroverts.

Masturbation is considered to be especially serious when it involves minors in Dumfries, Scotland. The law covers any person who "entices or allures, instigates or aids any person under 18 to commit masturbation or self-pollution." Both male and females can be prosecuted and sent to prison under this legislation.

Streaking in Great Britain was until recently punished under an old law pertaining to "indecent exposure." Penalties are ignored, for, according to the Home Office Committee, "Streakers are looked upon as no more than relatively innocent pranksters. They are presently able to avoid any stigma of a conviction for indecent exposure."

An odd piece of legislation in London, England, bans one person from taking money for touching the genitals of another person. This law was designed to help stop prostitution in London's massage parlors. But the police really have a tough time trying to enforce this particular law. These heroic bobbies have to muster their courage, enter a massage parlor, and bravely submit themselves to the sex act with one of the masseuses. "We do it for the community," declared one vice-squad detective. And yes, he did say that with a straight face.

It certainly appears that a man may legally molest a horse, a cow, a goat, or whatever he likes in Wicklow, Ireland. The authorities in Wicklow were notified of a fellow who was seen fondling a horse's genitals on the outskirts of the community. A policeman was sent to look into the man's "horsing around" and then wrote in his report, "After checking through my criminal code book, I was unable to find a charge to file."

Good old Aberdeen, Scotland! Women there were until recently prohibited from asking men to make love to them unless they were married—*to each other.* Nor could a man proposition a woman regarding lovemaking—unless the woman was his wife!

The Criminal Injuries Compensation Board in Great Britain is required by law to pay a predetermined fee of $1,650 to all female rape victims.

An old chastity law in Castlebar, Ireland, about says it all! It was passed some years ago in an effort to prohibit "crimes against chastity, morality, decency and good order."

Try to avoid taking a Sunday drive in or around Leeds, England, if you have any thoughts of making love. An old law there prohibits a man from asking a woman to fool around as he drives an automobile. (It must be okay to ask her while in a pickup truck, as the law specifies only cars.)

78

No unwed couples in London, England, are allowed to check into a hotel under assumed names for the purpose of having sex. An old city ordinance mandates a fine of up to £20 for people who "falsify a hotel registration" to obtain a room for lovemaking rather than sleeping.

Topless salesgirls are allowed to work in tropical-fish stores in Liverpool, England! One enterprising store owner hired a number of saleswomen to wait on his customers bare-breasted. The fellow reported an astounding increase in business.

An ordinance in Birmingham, England, actually required both male and female go-go dancers to wear bras while performing on stage. The law was later amended. Liquor Board members took into consideration the "recognized differences between men and women." It was decided that "no male go-go dancer would hereafter have to wear a bra."

Women in Whitehaven, England, can walk around the community with their breasts bared at all times. The police chief researched the law and found nothing to compel women to cover their breasts anywhere in his jurisdiction. He declared, "If they want to just walk down the street topless, that's their privilege."

79

Men in Sheffield, England, can freely and openly masturbate in the rest room of any store or business. There's no law prohibiting self-masturbation, but one male's having a hand in masturbating another is taboo. And females are never prosecuted; the ordinance covers only men.

Unmarried adults in Dundee, Scotland, are banned from going to one or the other's apartment or house to engage in lovemaking. Dundee's "Immorality Law" prohibits a single couple from going unchaperoned to any private place to have sex.

Don't go cruising down the streets in search of a prostitute within the city limits of Abington, Scotland. Those picked up for doing so will have their cars seized by the police!

Auto owners, beware when stopping over in the community of Bristol, England. Stern measures have been taken to stop couples from having sex while lying *under* their automobile! Lovemaking while inside a vehicle must be legal, as the law specifically bans making love only while lying underneath.

Restaurants in Glasgow, Scotland, are prohibited from having condom machines on the premises.

London, England, may be a great place for a vacation, but don't visit expecting to partake of the forbidden fruit. London has a law making it illegal to "patronize a prostitute." One might find it difficult to believe that such a law exists, given the incredible number of prostitutes openly doing business on the city streets, but this dastardly crime can bring a fifteen-day jail term and a substantial fine.

England has innumerable pieces of oddball legislation. No London prostitute is allowed to walk the streets and "publicly solicit or sell" her wares. But there's a major flaw in this particular piece of loony legalese: It doesn't cover homosexual prostitutes. They are allowed to "publicly solicit" partners for sessions of "deviant sex."

Citizens in Belfast, Ireland, can't let a single man and woman borrow a room in their home, or use their apartment, to have sex. "Nonmarital lovemaking" is forbidden under such circumstances. The loving couple can be taken to court and fined, and the occupant of the house or apartment can be fined and jailed.

Men convicted of first-degree rape or of forcing oral sodomy on a woman in Great Yarmouth, England, will pay dearly for their actions. Such a crime may well bring a punishment called the "incapacitation of the external male genitalia" by a surgeon.

It's illegal in Hollybush, Scotland, for condoms and other contraceptives to be seen by young customers in a pharmacy. Such "sexually stimulating" items can't be openly displayed on shelves because they might "encourage promiscuity."

Lovers in Bristol, England, aren't allowed to kick a dog out of bed just because the pet happens to get in the way during lovemaking. A dog, but not a cat, has the legal right in Bristol to observe sexual activities. But this is true only as long as the dog doesn't try to take an active part in the lovemaking!

Be careful when you travel through Tipperary, Ireland, and feel that old familiar urge. Any and all lovemaking between unmarried individuals there is illegal. Such activities are known under the law as "deviant sexual intercourse."

Couples who apply for a marriage license in Paisley, Scotland, are required to take a quiz on contraception. The law also says that they must be given a booklet explaining the subject. Both the quiz and the booklet are a mandatory part of getting the license and subsequently getting married.

82

The law in Hertford, England, gives a wife wide latitude in her relationship with her husband. She has the legal right to discard porno magazines, X-rated movies, videotapes, or anything else he might own of a sensual bent.

Having sex in a tomato patch is fine in Fullamere, Ireland. But no one, according to the law, is allowed to make love in any tomato patch located in a cemetery. So those who like a "tomato surprise" are out of luck, unless they do it at home in their own backyard garden!

It's a criminal act in Nottingham, England, for a woman to use her lovemaking talents on a man in an effort to break up his family. The law clearly says that a woman can't "fraudulently and deceitfully" lure a single man away from his mother in order to bring about a "clandestine marriage."

8

Loony Sex Laws from All Around the Globe

Men in Port Moresby, Papua, New Guinea, are required by local law to pay for their wives. The amounts are carefully spelled out in this loony legislation. The cost for a prospective "brand-new bride," believed not to have been touched by any other man, is the equivalent of $240 in hard cash, one bird, and five pigs. A widow or a divorced female goes for one bird, two pigs, and a sum equal to $30. "Twice married" females are a bargain for Port Moresby men. The law actually specifies: "Such women are of no commercial value."

Adultery isn't always a crime in Austria! It depends on how long a couple has been married. Anyone can play around and not be prosecuted so long as they've been married for less than a year. After twelve months of marital bliss, the same act becomes a serious criminal offense.

"Unfit for human observation" is what Italian law declares of many great works of art produced by such masters as Leonardo, Tintoretto, Michelangelo, Titian, and Raphael. The legislation bans the general public from seeing the little-known racier masterpieces of these and other artists. Florentine and Roman officials keep all of this erotic art locked up by order of the Italian government.

Spain appears to be quite liberal when it comes to some of its laws regulating lovemaking between consenting adults. The only kind of sex activities seen as illicit in this particular legislation are those "causing a public scandal"—making love in a public place such as a theater or on a bus or train, or having your sexual exploits publicized. Lovers who break this law can be fined up to 5,000 pesetas and be given a six-month prison term.

Virgins are no doubt at a premium throughout Greece. A man is prohibited from "seducing a virgin" by falsely promising to make the girl his bride. Any fellow who talks a chaste woman into going to bed with him and then refuses to marry her is in serious trouble! He must compensate the girl with a specified amount of money; such financial reward is deemed necessary to make up for the girl's "tragic loss of virginity."

No husband is allowed to assault his wife's lover within the city limits of Hamburg, Germany. He can't do this even if he catches them in the act, in his home, in his bed. Should a married woman decide to take on an illicit lover, and if her irate husband physically attacks that lover, the slighted husband can be arrested and given the equivalent of a $600 fine.

Fiji Island men who toil long hours in the gold mines are required by law to have a thirty-minute lovemaking break during their lunch period. Why? Simply because the miners are worn out at the end of each day and can't stay awake long enough to fulfill the physical needs of their wives.

Overcome with an urge to masturbate? Well, be extremely careful in Austria. Never masturbate with a friend! "Mutual masturbation" is said to be "an indecent act," but not necessarily an "unnatural act." Both masturbators will get a minimum of one week and a maximum of six months in jail for indulging in this particular activity.

It's against the law for any one person or couple to drive slowly through the Bois de Boulogne in Paris and continuously blink the car's headlights. Why? Because this is how French "swingers" signal other French swingers to let them know they're available for some bedroom fun. Couples can readily make contact with a single man or woman for a *ménage à trois* in this manner. Or couples can meet other interested couples for swapping or for an orgy.

Women can sunbathe topless or even fully nude on the beaches of Palermo, Italy. But men can't do the same! They'll be fined for doffing their swimsuits and sunbathing in the buff. Why are males discriminated against in this way? The law is clear: "The male anatomical conformation can become obscene, even unconsciously."

The city council of Tropea, Italy, passed a special ordinance designed to regulate nude sunbathing. No women who are "fat, ugly, or generally unattractive will be allowed to remove all of their clothing and lie naked" on the sandy beaches. The only nudes to be found on the beaches are "young women who are capable of exalting the beauty of the female body." Nothing in the law pertains to males who might enjoy basking in the sun while naked.

Norwegian beach guards carry black plastic bags with head- and armholes. These bags are given to women who are found to be sunbathing with their breasts exposed or while in the nude. Such women must slip

87

on one of these bags, or they will be placed under arrest and escorted from the beach area.

Prostitution in Zurich, Switzerland, isn't a crime. It's closely regulated by Zurich authorities. The local hustlers are allowed to work only in a specified red-light district. They also have to abide by a strict curfew: they can't solicit any customers between 3:00 A.M. and 8:00 P.M. There's now a move afoot, however, to change the curfew to 5:00 P.M. instead of 8:00 P.M. Why? As one Zurich politician explains: "Because of time factors and family reasons, many interested clients and especially businessmen would like to accept the prostitutes' propositions in the late afternoons."

There's an unusual law in effect on the Amboyna Islands. When it looks like a bad crop year is inevitable, the men are required to strip down after darkness sets in. They must then go to the plantations and masturbate. The crops are believed to be thereby fertilized with their semen.

Jerusalem is quite strict when it comes to dealing with couples who have the audacity to make love in the Church of the Holy Sepulcher. Both parties are given a fine equaling $610 and a sentence of up to six months in prison. Such a liaison, say the authorities, "desecrates a holy site and threatens interfaith harmony in Jerusalem."

Even graffiti of a suggestive nature can be a violation of the law in some parts of the world. Sensual poetry, graphic drawings, and profanity can't be put on the walls of a hotel room within the city limits of Heraklion, Crete. This type of activity is defined by law as a "public insult." Such graffiti always brings an automatic sentence of nine months at hard labor.

Women are banned from seeing the erotic art found in the ruins of Pompeii. One former house of prostitution is filled with small cubicles once used by the play-for-pay girls. Each room contains a stone bed for taking care of a customer's needs and a colored pornographic painting over the door. This picture is there for a practical reason. It eliminated all haggling since it clearly depicts the sexual specialty of the woman assigned to the room. Men may today see all of these erotic paintings for a tip of 50 lire. But not women, according to Italian law, for they aren't even allowed to step inside the building!

Norwegian homosexuals aren't ordinarily bothered much by the police. But apparently they could be locked up at the whim of a politician. The law is unusually vague. Homosexuals can be arrested and jailed or otherwise punished when it's "considered necessary in the public interest."

Some parts of rural Java are covered by a law designed to help increase the rice crop. All married couples are required to visit the rice fields after the sun goes down. They then make love in an effort to promote a better rice crop.

France repealed *all* censorship laws in 1974. But that country does have a law prohibiting hardcore pornographic films from being shown in any of its largest theater chains. Explicit sex flicks are still legally allowed, but they are to be shown *only* in the smaller, single-owner theaters. There are more than 200 of these throughout France.

Sweden may well be thought of by some as a wide-open sexual paradise. But it's not, at least according to the law that nation has regarding the use of coin-operated photomats. Such photomats are commonly found in train stations, bus terminals, and subway stations. Young women are prohibited from taking full-length, nude pictures of themselves in these photomats. On the other hand, photos taken by a woman who is naked from the waist down are perfectly legal. So are those taken by a woman who poses while bare-breasted. But full-length nude pictures are always a no-no. Nothing in this odd law mentions men taking pictures of themselves in the buff.

Don't try to give a cop a pornographic book or magazine when you are visiting Bar-de-Duc, France, and are stopped while driving down one of the city streets. A stiff fine equal to $1,000 can be given the driver of the automobile. Nothing in the law covers people who might instead be stopped in a truck, bus, or motorcycle. And as a sidelight, an additional fine is imposed on the publisher of the pornography, the person who actually snapped the photographs, and the author of the book. Each of these culprits is said to have "offended good mores," and they are fined the same amount as was the driver.

When the husband of a Tasmanian woman dies, the law requires that she wear her dead husband's penis around her neck. The women of Gippsland, in Australia, do the same thing.

An uncircumcised man in Samoa is prohibited from ever experiencing sex. No woman is allowed to become his wife. Nor can any woman consider having sex with such a man.

When a Turkish man marries a woman who isn't a virgin, he must by law spend three consecutive nights making love to her. Should a Turk marry a woman who is a virgin, the first *seven* consecutive nights following their wedding are to be reserved for love-making.

A particular four-letter profanity is considered to be an "obscene publication" in Marlborough, Australia, under certain circumstances. When is this the case? If a person has the word tattooed on his or her arm. Sporting such a tattoo brings a fine equivalent to $20.

Samoan law requires that a newlywed husband break his new wife's hymen with his finger. He must then show his bloodied digit to waiting relatives. Only then is he allowed to make love to his new bride.

Legislation was passed by the Pakistan National Assembly governing how much of a bride's dowry and wedding expenses could be spent. A dowry was limited to a sum equaling $500, and half of that could be spent on the cost of the wedding. All this was undertaken in an effort to thwart greedy bachelors who might ask for excessive payments in property or cash from the prospective bride's family.

Any and all acts of male homosexuality in Germany are punished by a maximum of fifteen long years in prison. Female homosexual activities, however, aren't against the law.

"Indecent acts" or lovemaking between two consenting females will bring a two-year prison sentence in England.

Look out, Spanish homosexuals! Spain's approach to homosexuality is tough. Authorities there will imprison any men or women who "habitually indulge in homosexual behavior."

It's still illegal in Greece to publish and sell the pornographic writings of the Marquis de Sade. This legislation is touted as a prime example of "ignorant medieval mentality" by a variety of Greek publishers. Yet the law stands.

Italian law prohibits women from viewing a specific life-size statue of a muscular man with an erection that is in Pompeii's famed House of Vettii. This attraction is open to all tourists—of the male gender, that is!

There is only *one* "unnatural offense" left in the criminal code of Victoria, Australia. Sodomy has been exempted, as have almost all other acts in the sexual realm formerly deemed to be illegal. A person can now do just about anything he or she wants to in Victoria—except have sex with animals. Bestiality is the *only* prosecutable sex offense left!

II

LOONY SEX LAWS
THROUGH HISTORY

9

Loony Sex Laws of the Ancient World

Early Rome was widely known for its Vestal virgins. Should one of the select virginal females inadvertently lose her chastity, the law was clear: The harsh penalty was a lingering death. The woman was buried alive in an underground death chamber! In this tiny room was a bed, food enough to last a few days, and a lamp. No other options were given the wayward young woman. A Vestal virgin who was foolish enough to give up her chastity was escorted to her death in an official procession. Plutarch described it thusly: "There is no spectacle in the world more terrifying, and in Rome, no day of comparable horror."

The law in ancient Sparta didn't allow husbands to have the "exclusive possession" of their wives. Sparta had what they deemed a progressive free-sex society. There was no need for prostitution. A man could have sex with any desirable woman, whenever he chose to initiate the act. A woman wasn't allowed to reject a man's sexual advances under any circumstances.

Ancient Greece also had its share of strange sex-oriented laws. A man could obtain a divorce for almost any reason, but he was prohibited from marrying another woman who happened to be younger than his former wife.

In early Roman times, lovemaking was against the law unless it was performed with the man on top!

Women in ancient Cyprus were required by law to earn money as prostitutes. This was undertaken in order to build a decent dowry for the man whom a young woman planned to one day marry. At one time or another, most women in Cyprus prostituted themselves. They otherwise would never have had money enough to garner a man in marriage.

No Christians in early Rome could indulge in sex on Wednesdays, Fridays, or Saturdays. Making love on any of these days was prohibited by law.

Ancient Babylonia was unique in its time with oddball legislation regarding sex. Every Babylonian woman was legally obligated to go to the temple of Myletta and prostitute herself for a minimum of one full year.

All fees earned were to be donated to the temple. Such prostitution was undertaken as a legitimate religious activity. According to the Greek historian Herodotus (484–425? B.C.), a woman was prohibited from returning home until a stranger threw a coin into her lap. She had to go with the first man who selected her; refusal was out of the question. The man would lead her to some nearby bushes for lovemaking. Only after they had had sex, and only after her year was up, could the woman go back home. Herodotus wrote, "Those who are squat and ugly may have to wait a long time. Some are known to have waited three or four years before the law was fulfilled."

Although the Ten Commandments banned adultery, old Jewish law allowed a man to take another lover if his wife proved unable to bear children. And a husband was allowed to take as his second wife the wife of his brother.

The following particular piece of Jewish legislation from ancient times is really unusual! Extramarital sexual intercourse was allowed if a married man "looking over a parapet accidentally fell onto a passing female, and accidentally effected a genital union as he fell." (In other words, never?)

Brothels in early Rome were required to close between dawn and 3:00 in the afternoon. The law even directed prostitutes as to how they should look when going to work. The women had to wear special clothing and dye their hair red prior to engaging in the business. And a special tax was even collected from prostitutes during the reign of the emperor Caligula.

Death sentences were readily handed down in parts of ancient Greece. For example, any free male Athenian of legal age who prostituted himself was in serious trouble if caught. The fellow was castrated and allowed to bleed to death.

The ancient Assyrians were thought to be quite civilized about lovemaking. But adultery and fornication (sexual intercourse between unmarried partners) were both punished in a number of unusually harsh ways. Apparently, it was up to whoever the judge happened to be on a given day. Some guilty parties were drowned. Some had their noses chopped off. Still others were castrated. Females often were given similar harsh judgments.

When a virgin became available in a Pompeii house of ill repute, the law required that an auction be held. The virgin was sold to the man who had the highest bid. She was his alone for the entire night.

In early Greece, a couple caught in the act of sex were in serious trouble! They were tightly bound together

100

and tossed into a lake to drown. If judged guilty but not actually caught in the act, the couple would be thrown in the lake but not tied up.

Prostitutes abounded all over ancient Peru, but none were allowed to live in any city. These women were social outcasts and were forced by law to live in the countryside.

Bordellos in Pompeii were the easiest thing in the city to locate. The law there required that all street signs near houses of prostitution be decorated with pictures of couples in a variety of sexual positions.

Again we come to Babylonia. There, any single male who seduced a single female was required by law to marry the young woman. If the fellow refused to marry her, the death penalty was imposed on him.

Any married Babylonian woman who was caught making love with a man other than her husband was guilty of a capital offense. When tried and convicted of adultery, she was immediately put to death by drowning. The man involved with her, even if he was married, wasn't punished.

Married women in ancient Greece were also given the death penalty when caught in bed with male lovers.

101

Yet married women were strongly encouraged by their husbands to seek out female sexual companionship. Lesbian love affairs weren't illegal in Greece, nor did husbands disapprove of such activities.

Christians in early Roman times weren't allowed to have sex for three full days before taking communion. Christians had to abstain from all lovemaking during this period. By the same token, lovemaking was prohibited for a period of forty days before Christmas and forty days before Easter. Sex was also banned from the day it was determined that a woman was pregnant until forty days after the child was born.

Pompeii was as cosmopolitan as Rome itself. Every brothel was required by law to have a price list posted beside every doorway. This was done to eliminate haggling over the established fees.

There were some places in the world with primitive marriage laws governing what took place after the wedding. Herodotus in the fifth century B.C. told how a Nasamonian got married. He wrote that the law required "the bride on the first night to lie with all the guests in turn, and each, when he has intercourse with her, gives her some present which he has brought from home."

102

According to ancient Greek law, any man in politics found to "lead a life of debauchery" had to be punished. How? He was prohibited from ever speaking in public before the People's Assembly. A lot of members of Congress might suddenly appear to have lockjaw if such a law existed in the United States!

Topless bathing suits for women reveal only what historians have previously observed—a female style that dates probably from times when one fig leaf was considered to be sufficient clothing. Prostitutes in ancient Crete, for example, always went bare-breasted in public; they were required by law to identify themselves by wearing a high-waisted skirt, an elaborate headdress, and absolutely nothing in between.

Sex for a mere donation in ancient Greece? Yes, in any Temple of Aphrodite! An abundant number of sacred prostitutes were there solely to make love to one and all. This was done in homage to the Goddess of Love. The law required that donations be given by satisfied customers. The women received none of the profits, however; the money provided the income needed for temple upkeep.

Fellows, be glad that you weren't a slave in Greece many centuries ago! Young male slaves, under ancient Greek law, could be legally castrated by their owner.

The legal code of the ancient Hebrews was clear on what constituted adultery. An adulterous relationship with a single, non-Israelite female wasn't against the law for a married man. But a married man having an affair with an unmarried Hebrew woman was considered illegal. The adulterer would inadvertently be violating the property rights of his lover's father. He was guilty of harming her father and punished accordingly.

A Hebrew man was prohibited by law from having a sexual relationship with a married Hebrew woman. The wayward wife and her lover, whether he was married or single, were equally guilty of adultery. They had each violated the Israelite husband's property rights. Both parties in the love affair were punished with an automatic death sentence.

Finally, any married Hebrew man could have an affair with a single Hebrew women whose father was dead. There was no punishment for adultery in this case.

All prostitution in Rome was open and above board. There were two basic types of prostitutes—those who were registered and those who weren't. The lower class of unregistered prostitutes (*prostibulae*) walked the streets in search of customers. A registered prostitute (*meretrices*) was required to file their name, age, place of birth, and any alias used in the business. The woman had to list her price, which, once registered, had to remain the same. They had to conduct all their business in a state-owned brothel (*Lupinar*). And the law required prostitutes to pay taxes on their earnings. Certain kinds of Roman citizens who worked part-time as prostitutes didn't have to register. These included professional dancers, actresses, and musicians.

Egyptian and Phoenician law required that certain prostitutes wear bright-colored "lipstick" when working. This was the way a harlot could subtly advertise and let prospective customers know that her specialty was in the oral realm.

Husbands in early Rome were able to obtain a divorce easily. A wife could be dispatched for not bathing with any degree of regularity, for fooling around with another man, or for "perverse and disgusting sexual conduct." A Roman husband, on the other hand, couldn't be divorced by his wife for any of these offenses.

A freeborn woman in ancient Athens couldn't be sold into the world of prostitution. Any man who forced such a woman into prostitution could be executed by the state. On the other hand, a single freeborn woman *could* be sold into prostitution if she had first been tried and found guilty of taking a married or a single man for a lover.

Having sex was banned by the ancient Canaanites whenever a friend or relative died. No lovemaking of any sort was allowed until the deceased's body was properly disposed of by the family.

All slaves, male and female, in early Greek history were forbidden by law to prostitute themselves.

After about 500 B.C., the penalty in Hebrew society for adultery was brutal for a woman. She was stoned to death—but her lover went unpunished.

No woman from an upper-class Roman family could work as a prostitute, but those who did were not punished too harshly. If one did and was caught, she was fined. Repeat offenders were quietly banished from the city.

Single women in Mesopotamia were required by law to go to the temple and have sexual intercourse with a stranger. This had to be done before they could legally get married.

Oral sex was outlawed as far back as 1500 B.C. The Hittites, a Semitic tribe from the Mesopotamia region, had a specific piece of legislation aimed at kinky sex. Their law specifically prohibited anyone from engaging in oral–genital contact in or out of the marriage bed.

Homosexuality ceased being acceptable under Justinian in the later Roman empire. The penalties were swift and exacting for both male and female homosexuals. After genital mutilation, homosexual males and females would be allowed to bleed to death.

Masturbation and sodomy were illegal throughout the Roman empire, as were adultery and any kind of homosexual activity. Anyone caught in a homosexual act or simply masturbating was stripped and publicly flogged. For the crime of sodomy or adultery, the participants might be sentenced to the amputation of their nose or cutting out of the tongue. Or they might be placed in a pillory and exposed to public abuse.

Ancient Egypt looked upon incest as not only an acceptable practice but a desirable one as well. Genetic concerns aside, the law allowed a man to marry his own sister and keep the family lineage "pure."

Adultery was a serious crime in almost all ancient societies, including Islamic, Roman, Oriental, and

Greek. In every case the law dealt severely with an adulterous wife. Her punishment for adultery usually involved scarring, maiming, or a horrible death. Philandering husbands were seldom prosecuted. But if a man was punished, he would have any or all of the foregoing, plus castration.

Any single woman who became pregnant in Rome during the reign of Augustus was in serious trouble. Men were forbidden by law to marry such a "wanton female enticer."

No *lupa* (prostitute) in Pompeii was allowed to ply her trade if she had bad breath. The law didn't allow customers to be insulted in this manner under any circumstances!

A young woman in Phoenicia was required by law to retain her virginity up until the day before her wedding. She would then be deflowered with a wooden phallus. Following this, the girl had to have sex with every unmarried man in her village. She was then handed over to her husband-to-be. This practice was eventually banned by one of Constantine's decrees after he demolished the Temple of Venus at Heliopolis and constructed a church in its place.

Barbershops in ancient Rome were quite often fronts for brothels. They were different from the usual houses of ill repute. The male employees were there solely to service and please male customers who were often interested in getting more than just a haircut or a shave!

Laws were passed in Athens of 500 B.C. that made prostitution a legal, government-run business. It all started when Solon, the lawgiver, decided that he needed more money to run his city. These state-run bordellos were first established in the Athenian port of Piraeus. All houses of ill repute were supervised by the police to ensure the customers maximum comfort and safety. And a law even mandated that large, specially trained dogs were to be kept on the premises at all times to frighten off potential thieves.

People in ancient Armenia were required by law, according to the Greek geographer Strabo, to "consecrate to the goddess, Anaitis, their virgin daughters. The [young women] take up residence in the goddess temple and therein prostitute themselves until they receive a suitable proposal for marriage."

No law against brothels in Pompeii? How about in the suburbs of other towns and cities throughout the Roman empire? Absolutely not! Legalized prostitution and houses of ill repute abounded, and they flourished. They were all run by government officials.

And they were heavily taxed as a source of revenue for the state.

Crete must have once been thought of as a homosexual heaven on Earth. Pederasty was authorized by law on the island. Aristotle wrote that homosexuality was legalized in order to stop a serious population explosion on Crete.

Naked slaves always accompanied women of breeding and stature to the public baths in Rome. The law required that these slaves carefully cover their genitals with a black leather girdle or a bronze plate.

Any Athenian man who used force to have sex with a woman was legally bound to marry her. Should she turn him away in anger, the fellow was flogged and then jailed.

Married women in ancient Rome who were caught in the act of committing adultery were required by law to take on all comers for a twenty-four-hour period. Interested men drew lots to see who would be the first. This law, according to Socrates the Scholastic, was in effect until the fifth century of the Christian era.

Adultery in ancient Greece was punishable with the death penalty. But seldom was this law ever enforced. Instead, the guilty parties were usually administered a beating by the husband. Or he might instead hire someone to handle the task.

A special law was directed at prostitutes who worked in the brothels of Pompeii. They had to dye their hair either blue, red, or yellow in order to be able to work.

Beautiful young women on Cyprus were required by law to prostitute themselves to foreigners who visited the island. Their earnings were placed upon the altar in a temple dedicated to Astarte. These youthful prostitutes would stroll along the seashore in search of paying customers. By the end of the second century, the money a young woman earned by hustling was no longer given to a temple. It was instead saved for her dowry.

10

Loony Sex Laws Throughout History

King Canute of merry old England was quite uptight about the devious crime of adultery. Any woman who was caught in the act with her lover had her nose and both ears cut off. The guilty male was merely banished from the country.

In ancient Siam, now the nation of Thailand, the king always shared his palace with more than 3,000 beautiful, handpicked women. The law specified that he be "attended by the ladies of the palace" between 11:00 A.M. and 1:00 P.M. And the good monarch was required to make love with one or more of his women every day of the year. Surely kings had a relatively short life span in Siam!

According to the law in early British times, wives were to be shared between groups of ten or twelve men. Brothers were to share their wives with brothers, as were fathers and sons. If the woman bore any children, the father was to be "the man with whom a particular woman cohabited first."

In Toulouse, France, Charles VI passed a law requiring that all prostitutes wear prominent white badges when in public. No woman for hire was allowed in the city without an identifying badge. This legislation went into effect so that a man would have no trouble finding the professional services he sought. And he thereby wouldn't accidentally offend any of the decent female citizenry with a proposition.

Men who dared commit adultery got the worst of punishments in England during the reign of Henry I. Adulterers were first castrated and then blinded!

Jewish men had it pretty rough in Venice in 1424. The law declared, "If any Jew be found with any Christian woman, or it be proved that he has lain with any Christian woman . . . the said Hebrew shall be subject to a fine of 500 pounds and shall spend six months in a lower class prison."

According to an old French law passed in 1635, all men caught pimping were sent to the galleys for life. A woman arrested for prostitution was to be "whipped, shaved, and banished for life." No formal

113

trial was required to convict the pimp and the hustlers.

Women weren't allowed to attend the theater while
wearing a mask in early-eighteenth-century England.
Originally, ladies wore masks in an effort to remain
incognito while watching a ribald play. Queen Anne
finally passed a law prohibiting the wearing of masks
in public. It seems that prostitutes were attending the
plays disguised as "ladies" and conducting a flourish-
ing business right in the theater—especially between
acts.

And in Tibet many years ago, the law required all
women to prostitute themselves. This was seen as a
way for them to gain sexual experience prior to marriage. Apparently in those days, no Tibetan male
wanted to marry a virgin. They preferred someone
who was already a seasoned lover.

In France, all prostitutes were exiled from the kingdom of Louis IX until public indignation forced a
change in the law of the land. The working people
demonstrated against the legislation because of the
"constant undersupply of whores." They felt it was
"becoming impossible for them to guard the virtues
of their wives and daughters."

In England during the Saxon era, adultery was a most serious offense. The lover was automatically sentenced to hang. The adulterer or adulteress was tied to a wooden stake and burned alive. His or her ashes were unceremoniously buried beneath the gallows.

Prostitutes in Milan were strictly prohibited from going inside a tavern or a roadhouse. Every prostitute was required by law to wear specific kinds of clothing so that everyone could readily identify them. Even the churches of Milan were given due consideration when it came to whores. No woman of ill repute was allowed to live within one mile of a cathedral.

In Sweden during the 1700s, young people were betrothed (engaged) and then legally allowed to sleep together as if married. Marriage was required *only* if the girl became pregnant.

Venice in 1405 had a tough law regarding adults who committed adultery. Both the guilty man and woman were forced to strip off their clothing and walk down the streets of the city while naked. And sometimes they were mounted on a donkey and paraded through the city. The ass, in Venice, symbolized lust!

Even religious events were protected from the taint of harlots in 1438 Venice. The law stated that "no prostitute . . . shall . . . permit her body to be touched upon the eve of the Nativity of Our Lord, on the day of the Nativity with its feasts, nor on the day of the glorious Resurrection and its feasts, nor throughout all the vigils and feasts of the glorious Virgin Mary, under penalty . . . of a fine of 10 pounds and 25 lashes, with eight days in prison."

Censure and condemnation in sexual matters were common occurrences in 1215 France. A law was passed that forbade the seduction of female students by male professors at the University of Paris and other schools. Such collegiate lovemaking was said to be an "exaggeration against good manners and decency, a scoffing against God and church, a worldly vanity, and a mad presumption."

In Spain of the seventeenth century, it was illegal for anyone other than a woman's husband to see her bare feet. A woman could freely expose her breasts, but the law considered a woman's feet to be sexual. It required that they be covered when their owner was in the presence of other men.

Renaissance paintings show the Madonna and other women with bared breasts. But artists were often prohibited from painting women with their toes or bare feet showing. Laws throughout Europe banned

bare feet in art because feet were said to be stimulating. They were seen as a "source of erotic desire,
suggestive and even sinful."

Certain young single women in England during the
reign of James I were guided by a most unusual piece
of legislation. These young women couldn't be seen
out in public unless their breasts were exposed to the
nipples. This was to be taken as a sign of virginity.

Polynesia once had a law outlining the responsibility
of the community for the successful deflowering of a
virginal bride. A nineteenth-century French anthro-
pologist reports: "On a signal from the husband all
the men present are to join together to form a line
while singing and dancing. Each in turn copulates
with the bride, who is lying in a corner on a platform
of stones with her head between her husband's knees.
The procession must always begin with the oldest,
and the least noble, finish with the great chiefs, and
last of all the husband." Variations of this unusual law
were also found in areas of Peru, the West Indies, and
New Guinea.

The Incas of Peru had a law governing what was to be
done with their most enchanting young women. Each,
when selected, became what was known as a chosen
woman. They were required to live a cloistered life

117

and remain virginal. Such beauties were given the official title of Virgins of the Sun.

Sodomy in sixteenth-century England was a crime punished by burning at the stake or hanging. The early British Ecclesiastical Courts had always been quite lenient in punishing subjects found guilty of sodomy. But by the time of Richard I, those convicted of sodomy were hanged, burned, stoned to death, buried alive, or drowned. Feelings about buggery have always run high in Great Britain. Sir Edward Coke (1552–1634), Chief Justice of the King's Bench in 1613, wrote for the court, "Buggery is a detestable and abominable sin, amongst Christians not to be named, committed by mankind with mankind, or with brute beast, or by womankind with brute beast."

In hot countries of the east, the sarong, hanging from the hips, became the sole legally acceptable garment of women and men alike. In Bali, a prim Dutch governor once passed a law requiring women to cover their bosoms. It didn't work! The Bali women went about their lives as usual until they encountered a Dutchman, at which point they then hurriedly lifted their sarongs to cover their breasts. In so doing, they exposed their pubic area to view. To say the least, the

118

law concerning covering the bosom was quickly re-scinded.

The T'ang Dynasty Empress Wu Hu passed a special law concerning one kind of sexual practice. The empress believed that a woman fellating a man repre-sented the supremacy of the male over the female. She insisted, therefore, that all visiting male dignitaries and government officials show their respect to her in a special way. Each was required by law to perform cunnilingus upon her when meeting. The empress would simply throw open her robe. The man would kneel before her and proceed to kiss her genitals.

Adultery was illegal in medieval Europe. Yet in France at the time of Charlemagne, it was impossible for a man to commit such a crime. Adultery could be committed *only* by a woman! The adulteress was thoroughly dunked in ice water and then left to be ridiculed by passersby.

Prostitution under Charlemagne's rule was treated severely. All prostitutes were given a death sentence. A man caught in bed with one could go free.

After the French Revolution, prostitutes in Paris adopted the filmy, flowing, classical Greek robe as their streetwalking attire. The muslin robe, a single thickness of sheer muslin, began to grow filmier. Soon the petticoat and chemise worn underneath were discarded for flesh-colored tights. Finally the bold Parisian harlots omitted the tights. The courtesans thus promenaded along the Champs Elysees in their search for customers. This outrageous attire was too much, even for France. The prostitutes' wearing of muslin robes was banned.

Passion, love, and sexual encounters brought on many serious difficulties during the Middle Ages. In eleventh-century Europe, a jealous lover or husband was allowed to harshly punish his indiscreet wife, concubine, or mistress. For example, he could legally murder the woman's lover and make her eat the fellow's cooked heart. Or he could, if enraged enough, make his former lover live with lepers for the rest of her life.

Many Native American warriors apparently had few reservations about engaging in sodomy. In the early 1880s, tribal law of the Nez Percé made it acceptable for a warrior to kill a man and then have sex with the corpse.

Homosexuality was outlawed among the Incas, and homosexuals were savagely punished. Garcilasso de la

Vega reveals in *The Incas:* "A careful search was to be made for the Sodomites and when found they had to be burned alive in the public square, not only those proved guilty, but also those indicted by circumstantial evidence, however slight."

Aztec law under Montezuma's leadership also condemned homosexuals. And the Aztecs strictly enforced their law. Their retribution for homosexuality was extreme. Lesbians were punished just as uncharitably as were their male counterparts and as were transvestites. For those caught in the act, the punishment was never less than death! Fernando de Alva in *Obras historicas* says that for those "acting as a female, they removed his entrails from the bottom, and tied him down to a log, and the boys from the town covered him with hot ashes until he was buried. . . . The one acting as a male was also covered with glowing ashes, and tied down to a log until he died."

The Mayans of the Yucatan had strict laws against adultery. Those who committed the indiscretion sporadically were ignored by the authorities. But those who made a habit of it received the death penalty.

One of the most fearsome laws dealing with prostitution could be found in the Venice of old. It was aimed at fathers and other relatives who forced young female family members to become prostitutes. Those who did this "shall be given over to serve in irons at the oars in our galleys, and shall be so condemned for two years, and in case they are not adapted to such service, they shall be cast into prison, where they shall be kept under lock and key for the period of two years, and thereafter they shall be banished from this City."

In 1254, King Louis decreed that all brothels in France were to be closed down. Prostitution was outlawed. Nothing changed!

In 1256, King Louis decreed that all brothels in France were to be closed down. Prostitution was outlawed. Nothing changed!

In 1259, King Louis decreed that all brothels in France were to be closed down. Prostitution was outlawed. Nothing changed!

In 1264, King Louis passed away, his edicts all ignored. When Louis died, the brothels were finally closed—but only for one full day of mourning.

Female actresses and dancers in nineteenth-century Europe were banned by law from appearing on stage in their bare feet. A few dancers were actually arrested under this law. The unusual legislation stated that exposing the bare feet "was a deliberate act of indecent sexual attraction."

Men were prohibited by sixteenth-century British law from going to bed "with a buttered bun." This simply meant that a man was barred from having sex with a woman who had just had sex with one or more other men.

French waitresses were required by law to double as play-for-pay hustlers when working in cafés called *brasseries des filles* in Paris of the Gay Nineties. There were at this time more than 200 such *brasseries* in the wide-open city.

Polygamy was once a popular practice among the people of Polynesia. Polynesian law stated that if a wife's brother had a daughter, she was to be a concubine of her husband.

Bestiality wasn't harshly punished in Italy. The Court of Rome simply viewed this practice as a means of making money. Authorities taxed anyone who was caught having sex with animals. The guilty party had to pay 90 tornesi, 12 ducats, and six carlini.

123

The French looked sternly upon any man or woman who had sexual relations with an animal. One man had sexual intercourse with a pig in 1465. He and the sow were burned alive together. Another man was found copulating with a cow in 1546. The cow was burned alive. The man was hanged and then burned. In 1550, a fellow was caught in the act of having sex with a she-ass. Both were slain on the spot and their bodies tossed on a pyre. And in Toulon, a woman who had been seen having sex with a dog was condemned to burn.

Any man who seduced a slave girl in Mexico in the sixteenth century no doubt hoped that she didn't get pregnant. If the girl died during childbirth, her seducer was required to become her master's slave for the rest of his natural life.

The Incas of Peru punished adultery with the same severity they had for the offenses of lying and laziness. Each brought a death sentence!

In 1266 Venice, a stern law was passed regarding citizens who let prostitutes conduct business in their homes. The edict noted that "certain ones in Venice are in the habit of harboring public prostitutes in their houses. It is hereby ordered that the said prostitutes be expelled from the said houses within eight

124

days. . . . No one in Venice is to be permitted to keep any public prostitutes in his house, under any pretense whatsoever." Violating this law brought a fine of 10 pounds.

England of 1777 had a special manner of dealing with female homosexuals. A lesbian was banned from "disguising herself in men's clothing and courting other women." Any woman who was caught doing this was locked in the pillory for ten to thirty days. This was done to expose her publicly. All other women were to ridicule her when they walked past. The lesbian was then given a six-month prison sentence.

Many of the western Native American tribes (e.g., Mandans, Nez Percé, etc.) had laws prohibiting their younger men from having any social or sexual contact with women in the tribe. They also had laws apparently sanctioning homosexuality. Youthful warriors were sometimes required to perform oral sex on an old medicine man or a crippled warrior. The young man was required to swallow the semen in the belief that doing so would transfer the other man's power to him.

Sodomy in sixteenth-century Italy was punishable by a small fine of 36 tornesi and 9 ducats. During this

125

same period, in France, anyone caught indulging in sodomy was burned at the stake.

Politicians in Venice were still passing laws relating to prostitutes and prostitution in 1358. Here's their law referring to pimps, who "are in the habit of daily following after prostitutes, living off the . . . evil doing of the latter, taking from them their money . . . threatening them and frequently beating them, when the said prostitutes do not wish to give up their money. . . . [T]he said youths alias procurers shall be subjected to a fine of 25 pounds and shall spend a month in a lower class prison and shall be banished for one year."

Venice, then widely known as a paradise for prostitutes in Europe, tried to do a turnabout in the sixteenth century. A multitude of stringent laws were passed in order to snuff out prostitution. Did it work? Evidently not so well, for a special edict was handed down to publish a booklet with this introductory message: "Herein is the catalogue of all the principal and most honored courtesans of Venice, with their names and the places where they dwell and the kind of pleasure each has to offer, and even the amount which must be paid by those gentlemen and others who desire their favors."

11

Loony Sex Laws in the American Colonies

It was serious business when any single fellow was caught in the act of having sex with one of the local girls in colonial Virginia. The fellow was quickly fined the sum of 500 pounds of tobacco for the crime of "fornicating."

Married men who took on illicit lovers were called "adulterers." A forfeiture of 1,000 pounds of the smoker's leaf was levied for committing this dastardly act! Alas, *only* the male participant was required to pay the unusual fine. Those adulterers who couldn't pay the fine were instead given a public whipping.

Adulterers in Maryland had an important choice to make when caught and convicted. They could pay a fine of three monetary pounds—or they could hand over 1,200 pounds of tobacco.

Any single fellow caught having sex in Maryland was also punished with a fine. He could pay 30 shillings for his indiscretion—or his fine was 600 pounds of tobacco. Individuals too poor to pay the fine were given a public flogging.

In colonial New England it was deemed to be illegal for citizens to partake of lovemaking on the Sabbath. Any child born on Sunday was refused baptism. Why? Because the authorities believed that a child was always born on the same day of the week he or she had been conceived, and Sunday lovemaking was strictly forbidden!

Every colony passed stern legislation outlawing sex between blacks and whites. In 1663 Maryland, law-makers noted that "divers freeborn English women, forgetful of their free condition, and to the disgrace of our nation, do intermarry with negro slaves." Under Maryland law, all the children born of such an "unholy liaison" automatically became the property of the slave's owner. And the white woman who gave birth to these children became a slave until her black mate died.

A stern 1676 Pennsylvania law punished men who "shall harbor, conceal or detain contrary to the consent of the husband any married woman, upon penalty of five shillings for every hour that such married woman remains under his roof; After [a] demand [is] made by her husband at the dwelling house where his wife is so harbored, concealed or detained."

Any Virginian who had the audacity to call a woman a "slut" might be sentenced to "one pottle of Milke per day at the cow pen until the last day of September." Or the offending fellow might be fined 30 pounds of tobacco. Then, too, the lawbreaker could be forced to stand in front of his church congregation for three consecutive Sundays while wrapped securely in a white sheet.

Adultery in 1642 New England was an extremely serious crime. When convicted of adultery, both lovers were required to kneel before the judges and implore them for forgiveness. Each had to willingly submit themselves, while stripped to the waist, to a severe flogging—usually ten to twenty lashes with a sturdy whip. Women *always* got flogged, but men could often avoid it if they simply paid a fine for their indiscretion.

The Dutch colony of New Amsterdam, today the city of New York, was often more severe in punishing sex offenders than was New England. Laurens, Yutie, Jan, and Geeje were apparently America's earliest "swingers." Laurens initiated everything by selling his wife, Yutie, to his best friend, Jan. This sale naturally resulted in Yutie's committing adultery with Jan. As a result, Laurens was sentenced to live with a "rope tied around his neck, and to be severely flogged; to have his right ear cut off, and to be banished for 50 years."

Jan, who committed adultery by living with Yutie, was sentenced to be "placed at the whipping post . . . to be banished 20 years and to pay a fine of a hundred guilders and court costs."

Jan's wife, Geeje, who had subsequently moved in with Laurens, was also charged with adultery. She was "to be conducted to the whipping post, and fastened thereto, the upper part of her body being stripped naked . . . and banished for the term of 30 years with costs."

Laurens's wife, Yutie, didn't escape prosecution. She was also found guilty of committing adultery, tied to the whipping post, flogged, and then banished.

Massachusetts passed a tough piece of legislation in 1705 prohibiting intermarriage between white women and black men. Sex between whites and blacks was severely punished. But this particular law apparently didn't apply equally to both genders. When a white man dallied with a black woman, his misdeed was usually ignored, and he wasn't prosecuted. But a white woman who had sex with a black man was ostracized and punished to the full extent of the law.

Connecticut had its own special punishment for anyone who dared play around outside of marriage. Colonists were prohibited from committing adultery, and the law made certain everyone knew about it when someone did. The penalty for getting caught in an adulterous situation? Up until 1694, having sex with someone else's marriage partner was automatically punishable with a death sentence! Replacing this chastisement was embarrassing hours of public exposure in the stocks or on the gallows and a maximum of forty lashes. Repeat offenders were treated more harshly. A branding iron was placed in some coals until it was red hot. The culprits were then held down, and the letter *A* was seared on the middle of the forehead.

Adulterers got off relatively easy in Pennsylvania. A one-year jail term was given to colonists who had been caught for the first time. Second offenders were often given a sentence of life in prison. And third offenders in Pennsylvania could also be branded on the forehead with an *A*, as were their counterparts in Connecticut.

131

Legislators in Virginia passed stringent legislation in
1691 that outlawed white people's marrying or even
making love with "Negroes, Indians or mulattos."
Any white colonist caught doing so was summarily
banished from the colony. The same was true for a
few colonists who went so far as to intermarry.

If a white woman in 1691 Virginia was caught making
love with a Negro or a mulatto and later give birth to
a "bastard child," she was forced by law to pay a fine
of 15 pounds sterling. If the wayward woman couldn't
come up with enough money to pay her fine, she was
sold into slavery, herself, for a period of fifteen years.

The Puritans in the Massachusetts Bay Colony held a
death sentence over the head of anyone who got
caught committing adultery. But few death penalties
were actually handed down for adultery in *any* of the
colonies. Public exposure in the stocks or a public
whipping was the usual penalty for such lesser charges
given to adulterers as "being in bed together," "lascivious, gross and foul actions leading to adultery," and
"filthy carriage."

Fornication first became a statutory crime in Massachusetts in 1692. Any single man caught making love
or "fornicating" was usually forced to marry his

132

lover. Or the illicit lovers might simply be fined and go their separate ways.

Fornication, or sex between single guys and gals, was considered a major crime in early Pennsylvania. Both of the consenting but unmarried adults were severely punished with a public whipping. A second conviction for fornication required even harsher floggings for both of the guilty parties. But the penalty for a third conviction was whippings three times each week for an entire month. Christians caught fornicating were required by law to appear before their church congregations and humbly beg forgiveness.

Branding a woman for daring to make love "with an Indian" was a popular punishment in the colonies. In this case, the letter *I* was seared into the guilty woman's forehead with a red-hot branding iron. However, a woman wasn't branded if she was a member of a socially prominent family; she was simply required to wear a red band on her arm for a period of twelve months. What was a man's penalty for "bedding down with an Indian"? There was none! Everyone simply looked the other way.

Jamestown, Virginia, had a critical shortage of women. Some of the lonely married men eventually sent for their wives in England. The majority of the single fellows diligently labored in the tobacco fields to make enough money to purchase a lifelong mate. The going price for a healthy, reasonably decent-looking wife ranged from 120 to 500 pounds of tobacco. But bachelors didn't appear to mind risking social ostracism for being caught in flagrante delicto with Powhatan Indian women. Jail sentences and some form of physical punishment weren't unusual for this violation of the law.

Divorce was permitted *only* on certain grounds in New England's Plymouth Colony. There were but nine reasons a divorce would be permitted. Seven were sexually related: impotence, bestiality, incest, bigamy, adultery, sodomy, and sex before marriage with a relative of the wife or husband.

In 1665, a Rhode Island woman was caught in bed with a man other than her husband. Tried and convicted in court, the adulterous woman was fined £10 and sentenced to fifteen lashes on her bare back. The flogging was to be administered in Plymouth. The following week, another fifteen lashes (stripes) were to be given in another public whipping, this time in Newport. The adulterer petitioned the court for mercy. The judge asked "whether she intended to return to her husband." She flatly refused to go back with him "no matter what the terms or the punishment." The woman was put in jail, and both whippings were eventually administered!

Some married women who were caught committing adultery in New England were tied behind a boat and dragged through the water. When nearly dead from drowning, they were pulled from the water and revived. This was followed by more dragging and reviving until her punishment was considered to be enough.

The most serious sex crimes in the colonies were rape, adultery, and sodomy. Each was punishable with a death sentence. Yet so commonplace were these crimes among the colonists that a death penalty was seldom carried out. Instead, the sentence might be reduced to flogging, branding, time in jail, or a fine. Or the guilty person might be placed on a platform in public with a noose around his or her neck. There they'd stay for many uncomfortable hours.

Sodomy was referred to by the Puritans as a "horrid crime against nature." They believed that sodomy broke the laws of man, nature, and God because this kind of sexual activity couldn't result in pregnancy.

In the colonies judges were known to conveniently forget that adultery inevitably involved two people—

not just a woman. Men quite often had fornication or adultery sentences reduced or even commuted. Not so with the colonial women. In just about every instance, judges threw the book at them. But, then, all the colonial judges were men.

Bestiality was a major issue confronting the settlers in New England. Cows, pigs, and other animals were put to death when a man was accused of having had sexual intercourse with them. The Reverend Cotton Mather exposed a close friend of his from Weymouth, a deacon who was a pillar of the church. He said that the man was "devout in worship, gifted in prayer, forward in edifying discourse among the religious, and zealous in reproving the sins of the people; everyone counted him a saint. . . . But it was found that he had been involved in buggeries [anal sex] for no less than 50 years." The deacon's wife and son gave testimony against him. The man's fellow church members forced him to watch as they hanged all of the guilty animals. Included were two heifers, two sows, three sheep, and a cow. Lastly, the deacon himself was hanged.

Black Africans were first sold in North America in 1619, according to John Rolfe in a report to London. It seems that a Dutch man-of-war dropped anchor in Jamestown harbor and had "brought not anything but

20 and odd Negroes." A mere eleven years later, it was discovered that some of the white colonists were mingling sexually with the blacks. A Virginia court record in 1630 cites Hugh Davis for "abusing himself to the dishonor of God and the same of Christians by defiling his body in lying with a negro." Davis was sentenced to a public flogging to be undertaken before a mixed gathering of whites and blacks.

Female slaves prior to the Revolutionary War could be whipped "for being a whore." The use of the word *whore* didn't mean that the slave was a prostitute. "Whore" simply meant, in the terminology of the day, that the girl was single and freely having sex, or married and having sex outside of her marriage.

Virginia in 1631 passed their first antiprofanity law. Any cursing brought a fine of one shilling for each word uttered. In popular use those days were words such as *prick* and *cunt*. So prevalent did profanity become that a new law was passed. This one required that the law regarding profanity be read at least every two months from the pulpit of each church in Virginia.

It was illegal in all the colonies for parents to have a child "too soon" after their wedding. The law required that both parents spend a minimum of ten days

137

and a maximum of sixty days in the stocks or the pillory. A family appointed by the church took care of the child while the parents were being punished.

Any young man who "carnally abused" animals in colonial times would be hanged for his sexual misdeeds. Thomas Granger of Duxbury, a servant, confessed to having had sexual relations with many animals. These included two calves, two goats, five sheep, a horse, a cow, and a turkey! Young women were not believed capable of this kind of violation, and therefore the law was aimed specifically at males.

12

A Potpourri of Other Loony U.S. Sex Legislation

California's Ventura County has a marvelous program mandated for pet birth control. A recent ordinance was devised by the Animal Regulation Committee. This loony law requires the purchase of a special permit. It is designed for cats and dogs that plan on fooling around. The cost? Only $10 for a license before quadruped sex can be construed as legal. But how do the felines and their canine counterparts know they now have to pay for sex? No committee member has figured out a way to tell them!

Tell this one to your congressman: Only sex between people who are married is condoned in the nation's capital. Yes, all forms of bedroom activities are outlawed in Washington, D.C., except for sexual intercourse between spouses—and this "must be undertaken only while in a face-to-face position." Husbands and wives have only one choice they can legally make—whether to be on the top or on the bottom.

While the nation argues with itself about the so-called sexual revolution, many archaic statutes still remain on the books. Adultery was once punishable by death in seventeenth-century Massachusetts. Thank goodness it no longer is! Useless, of course, the wronged person happens to come home unexpectedly.

Having sex just one time isn't a criminal activity in twenty-seven states. But these same states do outlaw couples' engaging in lovemaking on a regular basis while dating or while living together.

It's unclear in most states when "lewd and lascivious cohabitation" becomes common-law marriage. Those who want to live together without the benefit of clergy would do well to settle somewhere other than in California. But if a little hanky-panky is all you plan on having, then you're welcome. The Golden State has a law against "cohabitation," but none against "fornication"!

In Utah, living with more than one person at the same time is punishable by up to five years at hard labor. (As if *pleasing* more than one mate weren't already a form of hard labor!)

The various states are replete with what are known as sodomy laws. Georgia defines sodomy as the "carnal knowledge and connection against the order of nature, by man with man, or in the same unnatural manner with woman."

Florida's 1868 sodomy statute defines the crime as the "abominable and detestable crime against nature, either with mankind or with beast." Sodomy is further clarified in the law as "carnally knowing someone by the mouth or with the anus."

In California, as in Florida, no porno book store, X-rated theater, massage parlor, peep show, nude modeling studio, or other kind of "adult entertainment" business can be located within 1,000 feet of one another.

Houses of prostitution are sometimes disguised as legitimate massage parlors. In New Orleans, Louisiana, they are prohibited from locking their doors during regular business hours. Who could possibly get in if they did?

Men should not try to jog down the boardwalk while shirtless in Ocean City, Maryland—it's illegal! Topless males have been banned from the boardwalk. An indecent-exposure ordinance requires that all men wear shirts except when they're actually on the beach.

141

(What about topless women? Are they allowed on the Ocean City boardwalk?)

Highway patrolmen in Nevada are prohibited from driving a patrol car home after work if they're single and living with a woman. A spokesman in Carson City explained that the department wasn't saying a patrolman and his girlfriend couldn't live together happily every after. They were just enforcing the law, which in essence says, "Don't use your patrol car to get yourself home."

Not that anyone would really give a darn, but both skinny-dipping and lovemaking are outlawed along California's Trinity River. So secluded are some of the river's banks that transgressors can't be found guilty of "indecent exposure" for the crime of skinny-dipping. Nor can nature buffs be charged with "indecent activities" for merely making love in this remote wilderness area. But California authorities, for some reason, feel that such people have to be punished, so they charge them with "disturbing the peace" in the midst of uninhabited woods.

An old law in New Orleans states: "Any courtesan, bawd, lewd woman or similar inmate of a bawdy house . . . loitering in a house of prostitution who

142

shall be employed singing or dancing in any bawdy-house . . . shall be guilty of a misdemeanor."

In New Jersey, women-only clubs with male go-go dancers can be closed for presenting "lewd, indecent and immoral" entertainment. The dancing would have to "sexually stimulate" the female patrons at the club in order to qualify. A state liquor-control agent attended such a show and found it "intensely erotic." She readily admitted that the males dancing on stage had aroused her. The woman said, "It appeared quite obvious that many of the female patrons were similarly aroused."

Be extremely cautious in Indiana if you happen to own any jackasses or stallions. It's against the law to let these animals mate where people can see them in any city or town! There's a fine for anyone who gets caught: $3 for each day the animals are seen copulating.

One old Connecticut law banished the use of condoms and all other contraceptive devices.

In each and every state, it's illegal for juveniles to indulge in sexual practices of any sort. Then exactly what would eighteen- to twenty-year-old newlyweds do on their honeymoons in Wyoming? Play checkers?

143

Watch television? In Wyoming, they are considered juveniles until the age of twenty-one.

Florida is known for producing great football teams; however, some of the sex laws the state produces are rather strange. It still retains an old law, called the "unnatural and lascivious" act, covering a multitude of sexual matters. Hoping for the law's eventual repeal, a Deputy Attorney General in Florida acknowledged, "My wife and I violate this law constantly."

Better look after your male dog if you live in Danbury, Connecticut. Should Fido get a neighbor's dog pregnant, you, the owner of the male dog, are responsible. You're required by law to pay for the other dog's abortion if one is deemed to be necessary by her owners.

Animals in Los Angeles County, California, have a problem if they aren't able to read the law that prohibits them from mating within 500 yards of any church, school, or tavern. The penalty is a $500 fine and/or up to six months in prison. But the law isn't clear as to who does the prison time and who pays the fine. Is it the culprit or the culprit's owner?

It's strictly against the law for hogs to be found "mating on airport property" in Kingsville, Texas.

Any hogs caught doing this dastardly deed will be rounded up and auctioned off by the authorities. (That'll teach 'em!)

Just plain old fornicating can get a person into a lot of trouble with the law in various states. Here are a few of the penalties for partaking of the forbidden fruit while unmarried:

State	Fine		Prison Term
New Jersey	Up to $50	and/or	Up to 30 days
North Dakota	Up to $100	and/or	Up to 6 months
Virginia	$20 to $100	—	none
Georgia	Up to $1,000	and/or	Up to 12 months
Michigan	Up to $2,500	and/or	Up to 5 years

A person really doesn't have to worry much when making love in a parked automobile while in Coeur d'Alene, Idaho. It's almost impossible to get caught in an embarrassing situation. No police officer is allowed just to walk up and thoughtlessly knock on the window. Any lawman who suspects that sex is taking place must always drive up from behind, honk his horn three times, and then wait two minutes before getting out of his vehicle to invesitgate.

"Any person shall not tempt any man's wife," declares a sensible-sounding ordinance that was de-

signed solely to protect married women in little Buck-
land, Alaska. To further hinder a man from trying to
seduce a married woman, the law says, "A stranger
should not stop over night when the woman is alone."

Secondary schools in Carlsbad, New Mexico, aren't
allowed to have copies of *Webster's New Collegiate
Dictionary* in the classrooms. Only older editions can
be found on the premises. Why? Because the new
dictionaries "contain commonly used four letter
words" that have explicit sexual connotations.

The Los Angeles City Council recently passed a law
banning permits for expanding old motels that intend
to rent rooms for less than twenty-four hours at a
stretch. The law is designed to stop or at least hinder
prostitution in some sections of Los Angeles.

Women can pat men on the behind and get away with
it in Norfolk, Virginia. But let a guy pat a gal on the
rear and he's got big problems! It brings him a fine of
$150 and a possible sixty days in jail. (And perhaps a
civil sexual harassment lawsuit filed by the woman.)

Fairbanks, Alaska, has a rather strange law governing
the sexual activities of their native moose. Tourists
don't have to worry about inadvertently seeing a
moose mating with another moose within the city

limits. All moose are banned by the local law from "getting together" on any public sidewalk. Who, pray tell, informed the moose?

At least Florida is fair in its punishment of both sexes. It's illegal for unmarried "consenting adults" to make love anywhere in the Sunshine State. Chapter 798.03 of the Florida Code specifies, "If any man commits fornication with a woman, each of them shall be guilty." The penalty? A three-month jail term! According to this piece of legislation, lovemaking is permitted only between couples who happen to be married!

It's strictly against the law in Litchfield, Minnesota, for a couple to have sex in the back seat of a parked automobile while attending a drive-in movie. Seems it's okay if the lovemaking takes place in the front seat—only lovemaking in the back seat is specifically prohibited by the law!

The Lone Star State is currently considering a law regarding Peeping Toms. This new legislation contains three classes of exemptions to the Peeping Tom law: (1) one-eyed peepers, (2) peepers over fifty years of age, and (3) members of the legislature!

A prostitute "having sexual intercourse with a client for a fee" is guilty only of a misdemeanor in New

Orleans, Louisiana. But a prostitute "performing oral sex on a paying customer" is committing a felony! Section 14–89 of the City Code calls this kind of activity a "crime against nature." And such a dastardly criminal act requires a trial by a jury of six.

Thirsty after a long session of lovemaking? You'd better be careful while drinking that can of cold beer in Ames, Iowa. No man is allowed to take more than three gulps of beer while lying in bed with his wife or holding her in his arms.

Two or more homosexuals in Miami, Florida, aren't allowed to get together in any place of business. Why? According to the law, such activities just might "endanger or threaten the public health, morals, safety and general welfare." Alcoholic beverages of any kind, also according to the law in Miami, can't legally be sold to homosexuals.

It's illegal to advertise condoms in California, Wisconsin, and Arizona. Condoms can't be advertised in Arkansas without a special license from the State Board of Pharmacy. Kentucky, Idaho, and Montana all allow condom advertising—but only in pharmaceutical publications and medical journals.

New Jersey forbids anyone to advertise condoms "without just cause." Washington State prohibits the

148

advertising of condoms in a manner showing "when, where, how, or of whom" condoms can be readily obtained.

In the state of Illinois, condoms may legally be provided to an underage person "to whom the failure to provide such service would create a serious health hazard." However, women aren't allowed to purchase condoms anywhere in Indiana, or at least so says the law. Unmarried persons of either sex may not buy prophylactics anywhere in the state of Wisconsin.

The obscenity laws defining nudity in New Orleans are draped heavily in legalese: "Nudity is defined as the showing of the human male or female genitals, pubic area or buttocks with less than a full opaque covering or the showing of the female breast with less than a full opaque covering of any portion thereof below the top of the nipple or the depiction of covered male genitals in a discernibly turgid state."

One illustrious member of the Colorado legislature should have known better but obviously didn't. This master of loony legalese proposed an amendment during a major debate on a new antipornography law. He actually wanted to prohibit "any ultimate sexual act, normal or perverted."

149

The legislature of the state of Washington, pretending to be enlightened, has been trying to pass a bill to legalize prostitution. Every madam and each prostitute would pay a fee and then be licensed by the state. As might be expected of the members of a mighty bureaucracy, there was a catch. The prostitutes, according to the legislation, first had to offer "satisfactory proof that the applicant is of good character." Remember, though, this is the same state that passed a law prohibiting a man from making love to his wife on their wedding night if she happened to be a virgin.

Every state has loosely written statutes governing sexual behavior. The very acts being punished are seldom clearly defined. For example, Hawaii (Revised Statutes 768–51) imposes a $1,000 fine and a maximum of one year in jail for something it calls "lascivious conduct." Massachusetts (Annotated Laws 272–35) prohibits "unnatural and lascivious acts" in or out of the bedroom. It's illegal in Utah (Code 76–39–5) to act publicly in a "lewd, lascivious or obscene manner." Michigan (Statute 28.570 [2]) can penalize what it calls acts of "gross indecency" with a $2,500 fine and five years in prison. "Open and gross lewdness and lascivious behavior" are against the law in Vermont (Statutes 13–2601). New Jersey (Statutes 2A:115–1) has made it a misdemeanor to get involved privately in an act "of lewdness or

150

carnal indecency with another" person. Arizona (Revised Statutes 13–652) makes it illegal for anyone to commit "in any unnatural manner any lewd or lascivious act." And a "shameful or morbid manner in . . . sex or lewdness" is banned in Nevada (Revised Statutes 201.250).

State legislators in Baton Rouge, Louisiana, are extremely good at passing antipornography laws. To some observers, these people might appear to write their own brand of porn and call it legitimate legislation. At the end of this paragraph, you'll see that the correct number of blanks to make each word are provided. *The law itself spelled out each explicit word.* Here's Louisiana's wording of a bill designed to outlaw obscene bumper stickers: "No person shall operate a motor vehicle upon a public road or highway in the state of Louisiana when that motor vehicle displays whether by sticker, sign or painting, any of the following words that are lettered or written in a type or size greater than one eighth of an inch in height or width: (1) s--t, (2) f--k, (3) c--t, (4) t-t-, (5) p--s, (6) c--ks----r, and (7) any other word that is a compound or combination of any of these."

Pennsylvania retains an interesting old law concerning people who commit adultery. This piece of legalese, which dates back to the 1800s, prohibits a "spouse guilty of adultery from marrying the correspondent during the lifetime of the former wife or husband."

Like to partake of a little snuff while preparing to make love? If so, be mighty careful when with your lover in Warrenville, Connecticut. A local ordinance there prohibits a man or woman from using snuff during lovemaking—unless, that is, he or she has the permission of the partner.

And how about the old snuff-dipping law in Stark-ville, Mississippi? A single couple is outlawed from using snuff while making love in a room at any local motel. Nor can they smoke cigars while lounging around in the bed. (Well! Why bother renting a room at all?)

Sex of the oral variety often brings serious consequences to those who participate in this kind of "illegal" lovemaking. The penalties meted out in some of strictest states are as follows:

State	Penalty
Missouri	Not less than 2 years
Montana	Not less than 5 years
Alabama	2 to 10 years
California	Up to 15 years
Ohio	1 to 20 years
Rhode Island	7 to 20 years
Arkansas	1 to 21 years

Humorous laws aren't created by design but rather by a perfectly innocent misarrangement of words. Initially, the sentence structure probably sounded correct to the law's author, and the flub wasn't noticed until much later on. Ashland, Kentucky, has one like this. The law clearly speaks for itself: "No person shall knowingly keep or harbor at his or her house within the city any woman of ill-repute, lewd character or a common prostitute—other than wife, mother or sister."

III

Loony Sexual Court Rulings and Decisions

13

Loony Rulings and Decisions on Sexual Things

The Peeping Tom law in Mississippi applies only to males. When this law was challenged by a male peeper as being discriminatory, the Mississippi State Supreme Court ruled: "The legislature, by this statute, took note of the fundamental difference between men and women, and recognized that looking at persons for a lewd, licentious and indecent purpose is an activity traditionally ascribed to men rather than women."

A judge in Chicago, Illinois, ordered the impounding of the pornographic film *101 Ways of Love*. He said it was "definitely and utterly obscene." "Besides," he complained after having watched the film, "I only counted seven ways!"

A young man in Vancouver, British Columbia, Canada, was actually given a three-year suspended sentence for "possession of an offensive weapon." It seems the fellow had the distinction of getting three different women pregnant at the same time. He was ordered by the judge to avoid getting any woman pregnant for the duration of his sentence!

A young fellow was quickly acquitted of seducing an eighteen-year-old girl in Montes Claros, Brazil. The judge ruled, "Reality shows us that the real seducers are the daughters of Eve who sashay their way through God's world with their miniskirts, low-cut and see-through blouses and tight, tight pants, for the sole purpose of exhibiting their curvaceous bodies to attract the attention and the eyes of men."

A man was arrested for wearing a miniskirt on a heavily traveled street in Atlantic City, New Jersey. Even though the law prohibited anyone from wearing clothing "not belonging to his or her sex," the case was quickly thrown out of court. The judge ruled, "The city cannot dictate what a person can or cannot wear—there are a substantial number of women wearing men's clothes and dungarees."

Several naked female dancers were arrested in Los Angeles, California, and charged with performing in an illegal nude show. They all pleaded innocent, saying that a woman wearing shoes while dancing isn't really nude. Stretching reality to the absolute limit, the judge dismissed all charges, saying, "Stark nudity for public display is obscene. But when shoes are worn, the body can be said to be costumed and the display of the body becomes a performing art." Come on now, judge!

Ancient Greece's best known prostitute was Phryne, a play-for-pay woman who would have sex with her customers only in the dark. Arrested and tried for seducing a number of government officials, she was quickly acquitted after stripping in court. Why? Because she was able to convince the judge that "so perfect a body could not hide an impure soul."

Interested in auto-eroticism? A court ruling in Bologna, Italy, prevents the police from harassing prostitutes who happen to work out of their automobiles. The police aren't allowed to take away the driver's license of a prostitute just because she gets caught dispensing her sexual favors to customers in the back seat of her car. A judge, in dismissing such a case, said: "A prostitute can drive a car carefully and at the same time lead a scandalous life."

Some judges are direct and don't mince words. Yet they inadvertently tend to pick the wrong phrase to make a particular point. One instance is Chief U.S. District Court Judge Oliver J. Carter. Presiding over a trial involving a lesbian, the judge announced to her and a shocked courtroom: "I know you want me to put the finger in the dike for you and I'm not going to do it." In another instance, the judge again goofed when he informed a prostitute: "I'd like to get this case over so you can get out of here and go about your business."

A court in Munich, Germany, ruled that a prostitute's mugger had to pay her the equivalent of $1,100 in damages. Why? The judge calculated that the average German street hustler made $110 a day for her services. The prostitute in question missed ten days of work because of the mugging. Therefore, she must be paid $1,100 compensation for her "down" time!

Durham, North Carolina, passed an ordinance strictly regulating the operation of massage parlors in the city. In an appeal to the higher courts that was defeated, the judge, Hiram H. Ward, straightfacedly declared: "This case presents a touchy situation."

A court in Nashville, Tennessee, handed down a decision to padlock certain massage parlors throughout the city, whereupon the *Nashville Banner* misreported, "The court said the operation of such establishments has been declared to be a pubic [sic] nuisance."

Florida still has an obscenity law that was enacted in 1881. This law declares: "Any person who shall publicly use or utter any indecent or obscene language shall be guilty of a misdemeanor of the second degree." The constitutionality of this old law was challenged. The Florida Supreme Court upheld the law, but the justices couldn't bring themselves to spell out the words in question in their verdict. They wrote: "Let us first examine the language publicly used by the appellant resulting in his initial arrest, which is as follows: 'G-- D--- Mother F-----s, F------ Pigs and son of a B----.' Is this indecent or obscene language? We find that it is."

A waiter in a Pensacola, Florida, homosexual hangout "fondled the fully clothed customer in the pubic area for some five seconds with his right hand while holding a tray full of glasses with his left hand." When the waiter was taken to court, the trial judge instructed the jurors to determine if the man's conduct was "extremely indecent, immoral and offensive." The jury decided that it was! But the Florida Supreme Court ruled that this kind of activity didn't necessarily constitute "open and gross lewdness and lascivious behavior" in violation of the law. The Supreme Court then reversed the conviction, saying: "The term 'indecent' is difficult enough of precise definition, but the term 'extremely indecent' must certainly refer to

161

an act more outrageous than that perpetrated by the appellant. Additionally, who in the dark and crowded recess of the bar at two A.M. was 'offended'?"

A twenty-six-year-old British hustler in Southampton was arrested on the charge of "soliciting for prostitution." She had been seductively posing in a window with a red light in the background. A British magistrate dismissed all charges, ruling that the woman was "advertising, not soliciting"—and that there was a legal difference between the two!

Can a sailor's wife and children still collect a pension from the government if he dies of a heart attack while having sex with a prostitute? They certainly can if the dead sailor was a member of the Greek navy! A judge in Athens ruled that the sailor's demise was a "service-connected professional accident." The court's reasoning: "Referring to the naval profession, it is understood that this work requires long periods of separation of a seaman from his wife and family, and the need for his recreation in areas he feels deprived."

And here's another classic! A circuit court judge in Grant County, Wisconsin, placed a twenty-year-old farm worker on three years' probation and gave him a ninety-day work-release sentence in a sexual assault case. When passing sentence, the judge remarked that the *five-year-old victim* was "a promiscuous young lady" and "unusually sexually promiscuous."

"Female breasts," per the Arizona Supreme Court, don't constitute "private parts" under the state law.

A young fellow pleaded guilty to stealing a package of condoms from a drugstore in Drummondville, Québec, Canada. The prosecutor explained to the judge that the theft didn't appear to be premeditated. With a slip of his tongue, the judge responded by asking if he felt the condoms had been stolen "on the sperm of the moment."

A sixty-one-year-old resident of Messina, Italy, made love to his twenty-year-old sweetheart. The old gent was so enthused afterward that he ran outside in the middle of the night to celebrate. He began to ring the bell in an empty church. His wife angrily filed a "public nuisance" complaint. But a civil tribunal refused to penalize the elderly fornicator or his sex partner. It was ruled to be "not a crime for an old man to celebrate a successful sexual interlude by ringing a church bell, whatever the hour."

A married woman who's having an affair isn't obligated, said a Michigan court, to warn her lover of danger from her jealous husband. In this case, a

163

woman was fooling around on the side and her husband was aware of the hanky-panky. When she asked her husband for a divorce, he shot and wounded her lover. After recovering, the fellow divorced his wife and married his former lover. He then sued her for compensation for the injuries he'd received from being shot by her former husband. The judge ruled that a woman having an affair wasn't obligated to warn her lover of her husband's potential violent reaction to their illicit sexual activities. He concluded, "A married woman has no duty to urge her husband to seek psychotherapy or spiritual guidance for the benefit of the man with whom she is having an affair."

Two men were sitting in a parked automobile on a deserted residential street in Honolulu at 3:30 A.M. They were arrested on a charge of "open lewdness." But the Supreme Court of Hawaii subsequently ruled: "Two men engaged in oral sex in public can't constitute the crime of 'open lewdness' if someone else isn't likely to see them." Besides, said the court, "the police officers admitted they couldn't see a thing until they illuminated the inside of the vehicle with a flashlight."

A judge in Lexington, Kentucky, banned the showing of pornographic movies at the Dixie Gardens Drive-In because of driving safety. The court ruled: "The blatant sexually explicit nudity caused massive traffic jams on adjacent Interstate 75."

There'll be no topless sunbathing on the lovely beaches of the Sunshine State. Anyone caught sunbathing without a bikini top will be apprehended for "disorderly conduct." Justice Joseph Boyd of the Florida Supreme Court noted that "public nudity has [always] been considered improper." He then quoted from the book of Genesis to prove his point: "And the eyes of them both were opened, and they knew that they were naked; and they sewed fig leaves together, and made themselves aprons."

A thief in Lansing, Michigan, was angered at his sentence of a minimum of thirty months to five years in the penitentiary. He unzipped his pants, pulled out his penis, and began cursing the judge and everyone else in the courtroom. The thief was given a new minimum sentence of forty years by the irate judge. (This additional time was later set aside by the Court of Appeals.)

A man in Durban, South Africa, was charged with attempted murder for shooting an air rifle at a couple of circling hang-glider pilots. It came out in court that his wife had been sunbathing in the nude atop his garage roof. The hang-glider pilots flew extremely

165

low over the roof in order to get a better look the woman, and one shouted a sexual suggestion to her. The furious husband began firing away. The case was dismissed as "frivolous and totally lacking in merit."

A court in Germany blocked the request of an unmarried convict who wanted an "escorted leave to visit a brothel." The inmate's petition was turned down because, said the judge, officers "would have to supervise to the fullest degree any sexual activity." And since the prisoner would be handcuffed, officers "might be called upon to render assistance." The judge further made note of the fact that the "inmate's long continence would probably reduce the entire procedure to a few seconds"!

14

Loony Punishments for Loony Sex Violations

Upon a prostitute's conviction in a Los Angeles, California, court, the judge sentenced her to spend three days in front of City Hall while carrying a sign reading, "I've been convicted of prostitution." The young woman willingly followed the judge's decree rather than spend time in jail. In obediently carrying out the court's mandate, the enterprising prostitute handed out business cards to interested men who happened to see her in passing.

A doctor in Indianapolis was married for ten years when his angered wife filed a complaint of sodomy against him. He was charged with breaking a nine-teenth-century Indiana law against the "abominable and detestable crime against nature with mankind or beast." The wife admitted to having willingly partici-pated in various oral sexual activities. Before going to trial, the wife tried to drop the charges. But the

Attorney General's office refused. Her husband's bedroom antics constituted a crime against the state! The doctor was convicted and given a prison sentence of two to fourteen years.

According to the *Quincy Herald*, in Quincy, Illinois, a fifty-seven-year-old man was given a fine of $10 in a circuit court for "having a loose protruding member."

A young man was notified to report to his draft board in Baton Rouge, Louisiana. He instead wrote back telling them he was a homosexual and should be exempted from military service. The draft board responded, saying some sort of proof was required. So the guy sent a package of explicit photographs of himself and some boyfriends in action. The result was a hearing in a San Francisco Federal Court. He was fined $250 and placed on five years' probation for the felony of sending "obscene, lewd, indecent, filthy and vile matter" through the mails.

A judge in San Francisco, California, gave a prostitute what may have been the highest bond ever imposed in a court of law. The judge was thoroughly frustrated by a police practice of routinely releasing misdemeanants in order to alleviate jail overcrowding. So he decided to do something about the problem and set the hustler's bail at an astounding *$5 billion!*

168

The downtown area of Bangor, Maine, was the site of a rather unusual unlawful sexual activity. A man was caught in the act of flashing in front of a major department store. He was arrested for "public indecency." Was he rudely exhibiting himself to some hapless female as she window shopped? Not hardly! The fellow was excitedly exposing his sexual equipment to, of all things, a display of Barbie dolls in the store's window. An unsympathetic judge gave the man five years in the penitentiary.

A woman in Denver, Colorado, was convicted of running a house of ill repute. In a unique decision, the judge gave the thirty-nine-year-old madam a ninety-day sentence. She was remanded to the "care, custody and control" of the Convent of the Good Shepherd, a Catholic order devoted to assisting wayward women. The defense attorney commented, "It's not unlike what Hamlet said to Ophelia: 'Get thee to a nunnery, go.'"

Seventeen men between the ages of seventeen and fifty-two were caught propositioning a policewoman posing as a prostitute in Lansing, Michigan. Each man was sentenced to write an essay on how his personal life had been affected by his conviction.

A high government official in Nepal was found guilty of bigamy! "Ho hum!" said the judge who heard the case. He simply smiled and fined the man twenty-five cents.

A judge in Madison County, Alabama, made a practice of trading his influence for women's sexual favors. One young lady found a way to stop her brother from being criminally prosecuted: She simply made love with the judge. Another woman, being tried on bad-check charges, also escaped prosecution by making love with his Honor. The judge was finally caught. He was tried and convicted for his unethical sexual shenanigans and was sentenced to three years in prison.

A cashier in a St. Louis, Missouri, adult book store sold a pornographic magazine to an undercover cop. Charged and taken to court, this fellow was fined an astounding $25,000. Even more incredible was his sentence—fifteen years in the penitentiary!

Two women fellated five adult men, all of whom happily consented, at a bachelor party in Providence, Rhode Island. The women were arrested and charged under an old 1896 statute that made the "abominable and detestable crime against nature" a very serious felony. Violators of this antique legislation could be punished with a *minimum* seven-year stretch in the penitentiary. The judge, recommending that the women appeal the case, suspended all of the sentence except for ninety days. Calling the statute archaic, he found it "difficult [to believe] that sexual activity between consenting heterosexuals in private concerning fellatio is still criminal in Rhode Island [and that] for 20 years the legislature has carved out no exceptions." By the way, none of the five men involved were prosecuted under the 1896 statute!

A young Maryland fellow received a five-year suspended sentence because of his involvement in an "unnatural and perverted sexual practice." It seems that this man got caught with a woman who was willingly performing fellatio on him. Since fellatio is sodomy, reasoned the Court of Special Appeals, and since sodomy is against the law in Maryland, the man's conviction was upheld. The judge admitted that the state's "unnatural and perverted sexual practices" law is not only archaic—it's unreasonable! Yet, he pointed out that a change in this law would have to be made by the legislature and not the courts. In this case, only the man involved was prosecuted. The woman wasn't charged with breaking any law.

Lack of sex in a marriage is always grounds for an annulment for both husband and wife. However, a wife can sue for a divorce on the grounds that a husband is oversexed. How many times a married

171

couple should or shouldn't have sexual relations was decided by the Supreme Court of Minnesota. The panel of judges upheld a lower court ruling that maintained a forty-two-year-old married man's need for sex an average of three or four times each week wasn't normal. This constituted, said the court, an "uncontrollable craving for sexual intercourse" by a husband. This father of six was branded a "criminal sexual psychopath" by the court and incarcerated in a mental institution!

A man in Marietta, Georgia, picked up his shotgun and went out to check on his daughter and a young fellow who were sitting in the car parked near the house. He found the eighteen-year-old boy behind the wheel with his pants unzipped and his penis exposed. On trial for murder, the father explained how he "just went berserk." The prosecutor told how the man had taken "a cold-blooded, calculated shot into a part of the boy which [he] saw and thought was the source of the problem." The murder trial went on for two days. A jury of three women and nine men deliberated only three hours before acquitting the man.

A twenty-seven-year-old prostitute was convicted under the Mann Act in Pittsburgh, Pennsylvania. It seems she had transported two other women across state lines "for immoral purposes." The prostitute got three years' probation from a sympathetic federal judge who commented, "I have no feelings of antagonism for the honest prostitute." He went on to say, "I feel absolutely no sympathy for the pimping side of the coin." Her pimp was sentenced to thirteen months in the penitentiary.

A married couple, both seventy years old, came to Sioux Falls, South Dakota, from Nebraska in hopes of generating more business. He was a pimp, his wife a prostitute. They made a serious error in judgment. A sheriff's deputy, propositioned at the going price of $10, quickly made an arrest. The couple was booked on charges of "soliciting," and "transporting a woman for purposes of prostitution." Plea bargaining reduced the charge to "lewdness." The old couple agreed to leave Sioux Falls and never to come back after paying a fine of $200.

A man in Canada was arrested on a charge of rape and "gross indecency." The rape charge was quickly dropped because the woman had consented to both sexual intercourse and cunnilingus. The judge spoke to the jurors just before they left the courtroom to consider the "gross indecency" charge: "Well, can you think of a much more grossly indecent act? . . . Frankly, gentlemen, I had to get the dictionary to know what it was about. I venture to say that most of you are the same. . . . A dirty, filthy practice such as this that is resorted to by no one but by sexual perverts is surely an infringement of the criminal code." The jury found the defendant indeed guilty of "gross indecency." He was given three years in prison. The case was appealed. Here, again, the new judge appears to have unfairly influenced the jury: "The accused's behavior was unnatural and depraved and violated the common standards of conduct accepted by the people of our land, and it is our view that Canadians are not prepared to condone such acts as falling within acceptable standards of behavior." And again, a guilty of "gross indecency" was returned, and the fellow's three-year sentence was upheld!

15

Loony Lawsuits Over Courtship, Seduction, and Other Matters of the Heart

A young couple in Pilot Mound, Iowa, were sitting close together on a couch in the girl's family's living room. They were in the midst of a deep kiss when the young lady's father barged into the room. Furious at seeing the partially disrobed couple, he began to scream at the loving twosome. The boyfriend, enraged by what he considered to be an untimely interruption, hastily grabbed the unwelcome intruder and gave him the bum's rush out of the house. The girl's father brought a damage suit against his daughter's sweetheart. He complained vocally to the court, "A man's home has been his castle ever since this country began. In a democratic republic like we have, that's elementary. It always has been and it always will be." But the judge disagreed and responded with a precedent even more elementary. Said his Honor, "Courting is a public necessity. It must not be interrupted. The law of this state will hold that a parent has no legal right in a room where courting is afoot. Case dismissed!"

A man in Joplin, Missouri, was awarded $25,000 in damages from the estate of his former wife's lover. It seems that his wife and the deceased had previously had an adulterous relationship. Therefore, her sweetheart was liable under Missouri law, even though he was now dead. The judge ruled, "The wrongful invasion of a husband's marital rights has no precise market value and its valuation is a matter about which reasonable persons may and do differ."

A swain in Decatur, Alabama, was jilted by his lover. She added insult to injury by adamantly refusing to return the diamond engagement ring. When the boyfriend appealed to the courts, the judge ruled that his sweetheart could indeed keep the ring. It was to be considered as "equitable and just reimbursement for the costs of lighting and heating her parlor and bedroom during the romance."

Here's one for frustrated married women who complain of not getting enough sex. A thirty-year-old British mechanic filed suit for divorce because his wife would allow him to make love to her only once each week. The divorce request was denied because, in the words of the judge, "It seems quite impossible for any court to find that the refusal by a wife to have sex more often than once a week is unreasonable."

An unmarried and pregnant mother in Paterson, New Jersey, sued the father of her children for support payments. But Municipal Court Judge Ervan Kushner surprised everyone in his courtroom when he turned the tables on her. He ordered that charges against the woman and her lover be filed under the state's 1790 fornication law. This old legislation simply outlaws unmarried people from having sexual intercourse. Why did the judge take such action? Because, he explained, "I saw a crime being committed when a single woman walked into my court pregnant." Both the woman and her lover were convicted!

A man in Huntington, West Virginia, was jubilant when he finally won the hand of his lover. But this marvelous feeling of elation was somewhat tempered when his defeated rival hauled him into court. The judged ruled in favor of the jilted lover! The fellow who ended up marrying the woman was ordered to pay $300 to his competition for "wasted courtship expenses."

Here's a born loser from Bloomington, Illinois! This guy never stood a ghost of a chance. He was clobbered by two lawsuits. One was filed by his wife, who accused him of being impotent. The second was filed by the maid, who accused him of seducing her. He lost both cases!

And then there's the great lover from Atlanta, Georgia, who was the defendant in a unique paternity suit. The fellow pleaded that, although he was the father of one of the plaintiff's twins, he certainly wasn't the father of the other!

A young woman in San Antonio, Texas, won damages in her "breach of promise" lawsuit. Her lover protested that he'd never proposed marriage, yet the judge ruled that there was "strong evidence of a proposal." And what exactly was this "strong evidence?" The hapless guy had mailed his lover a newspaper clipping with this headline: "Love, the Conqueror."

A woman in Provo, Utah, won a $6,000 judgment for "breach of promise." Why? Because her lover died before their wedding day.

Kisses can be a costly pastime. A man in Little Rock, Arkansas, for instance, was sued by his lover for giving her a kiss she didn't particularly want. The court awarded the woman a $1,500 settlement. Another guy from Rawlins, Wyoming, was sued for merely puckering his lips at a woman as she shopped in a department store. He ended up settling out of court for a $300 payoff. And a farmer in Pendleton, Oregon, was sued when, while he was in the throes of lovemaking, his impassioned kiss loosened his fiancée's gold filling.

But the hard-luck chamapion was a Cassanova from Brooklyn, New York. This arrogant fellow had mastered the fine art of seduction. Through months of intense romance, he tantalized his lover with the tinkle of wedding bells. But the bells always seemed to be tinkling in the far-distant future. At long last, despairing of ever marrying him, the young woman sued her boyfriend for "breach of promise." At the trial, the judged asked her: "Did the defendant ever actually promise to marry you in writing?" "Oh, gracious no!" she readily conceded. "Did he promise you orally?" "No," she admitted. "Then how *did* he promise you?" demanded the judge. "By implication," the jilted party said firmly. "He would hug and kiss me in public." That did it! "The gleam of the eye and the conjunction of the lips," ruled the judge solemnly, "when frequent and protracted, is a sufficient promise." It cost Casanova $25,000.

After completing her testimony in a Chicago, Illinois, sexual harassment trial, a young woman blushingly asked the judge for permission to make a correction for the record. In her turmoil, she explained, she had unintentionally given her bust measurement instead of her age.

Hagerstown, Maryland, was the site of a paternity suit. The judge listened attentively to both sides in a case brought by a secretary against her boss. When it came time to announce his verdict, the judge pulled a cigar out of his pocket. He handed it to the defendant with a flourish. "Congratulations!" his Honor said. "You've just become a daddy!"

A southern belle, unmistakably beyond forty, appeared in a Vicksburg, Mississippi, courtroom as a witness to a crime. As she stepped to the stand, the clerk raised his hand. "Madam—" he began. But the judge hastily intervened. "I'll swear in this witness myself," he said. With a gallant bow, he asked the woman, "How old are you?" "Twenty-six," she replied coyly. "And now," continued the judge, "do you solemnly swear to tell the truth, the whole truth, and nothing but the truth, so help you God?"

Newlyweds from Norwich, Connecticut, made a trip to Honolulu, Hawaii, for their honeymoon. Alas, the bed in their hotel room collapsed during their wedding-night activities. The husband sued the hotel for millions. He was awarded a $905 settlement!

Damages of $407,000 were awarded to the Canadian owner of a pedigree Holstein bull named Pioneer Emperor Arab. It seems that this prize bull was in Chester, England, relaxing in a field while under orders from a veterinarian to refrain from fooling around. A herd of cows from a nearby farm strayed into Arab's private field. According to a local newspaper: "Clearly recognizing his duty, Arab nearly worked himself to death." Arab became extremely ill because of his overtaxed sexuality and had to be destroyed. A $407,000 judgment was issued against the owner of the herd of wayward cows.

A young fellow in Boston, Massachusetts, was held in jail for one month on a rape charge. He later brought suit against the city and was offered a handsome out-of-court settlement. Why? Because the Boston police had never bothered checking his alibi. At the time of the purported rape, he was actually at a wedding reception along with more than one hundred other people. Whose reception? His and his new bride's. They had just gotten married!

A married woman in Phoenix, Arizona, met an Episcopal priest in a confessional. She subsequently had

181

an affair with the man of God. Upon discovering his wife's indiscretions, her irate husband filed an "alienation of affection" suit in an effort to collect damages. He contended that the bishop and the diocese were financially liable for the priest's conduct. But the judge disagreed and ruled: "If the servant has turned aside from the master's business to pursue a mission of frolic of his own, he is clearly not engaged in the master's business so as to create liability upon the master for his wrong."

A woman in Ogden, Utah, filed a $250,000 "alienation of affection" lawsuit against her neighbor. The "other woman" was charged with "hustling" her husband. The wife's suit contended that her husband took the neighbor to Hot Springs, Arkansas, when he went for his annual visit. What's so unusual about all this? The husband was ninety years old, his jealous wife eighty-two, and his lover a mere eighty-one!

A thirty-year-old man from Delphos, Kansas, went into a medical clinic for a simple circumcision. He ended up with a vasectomy by mistake! He sued the clinic and received an undisclosed amount of money in an out-of-court settlement.

A man in Cleveland, Ohio, who had a history of heart trouble filed a $35,000 damage suit against his ex-wife and her lover. The ex had allegedly sent him a video of her making love with the man. Her intent, he claimed, was to bring on another heart attack. The fellow did, upon watching the video, experience shortness of breath and chest pains.

So you've always wondered about morticians and "stiffs"? A twenty-three-year-old female apprentice mortician in Sacramento, California, allegedly sexually molested a male corpse. The fellow's mother sued and was actually awarded $142,000 in damages. Testimony in court revealed that the mortician may have molested as many as forty other bodies while employed at the funeral home.

A New York dentist administered general anesthesia to one of his female patients. The woman grabbed him firmly by the testicles as she went under. Alarmed more than just a little, the dentist had to break one of the woman's fingers in order to extricate himself from her eye-watering grip. She in turn sued and was awarded $500 in damages! This is the true meaning of "a real ballbuster"!

A young Sicilian woman was married in New York City. The very next day her furious husband unceremoniously dumped his new bride on her uncle's stoop and ran off. He told all who would listen that his wife hadn't been a virgin on their wedding night. His public accusations spread through the Sicilian neighborhoods as far away as New Orleans and California. Because of this, and the fact that the girl and her family became social outcasts, a sympathetic court awarded the young woman $250,000 in damages.

A woman in Seattle, Washington, brought a frivolous lawsuit against a large corporation. She claimed that the company failed to warn her that her husband, an employee of the company, was having a love affair with a woman on the job. A state court of appeals threw out the lawsuit, saying the company "owed no duty to its employees' spouses to monitor and safeguard their marriages and, therefore, could not be held liable in negligence under any set of facts."

An electrical contractor in Orlando, Florida, sued a customer over an unpaid $625 bill. The woman testified that "the whole deal was to be wiped out with one sexual experience." This was not acceptable to the judge. He ruled the woman still owed the contractor $377. Why? Because the sex act was "performed for the enjoyment of both parties." The judge added, "The woman who came to court in a baggy man's shirt and overalls made little or no attempt to convince the court of the value of her personal services if they were to be considered part of the evidence."

A judge in Portsmouth, Maine, described a handsome twenty-seven-year-old man as a "love slave of the defendant." The woman, a thirty-eight-year-old owner of a pizza parlor, claimed that she had generously supported her young employee in lieu of paying him a salary. But the judge saw it differently. He awarded the fellow $13,810 in back pay despite the woman's pleas to the contrary.

An affair with another man's wife can sometimes be costly in more ways than one. For example, a fellow in Winston-Salem, North Carolina, initiated a romantic *tête-à-tête* with a married woman. She and her husband eventually divorced as a result of the shenanigans. The divorced husband turned around and brought suit against his ex-wife's lover for damages. The judge ruled in his favor, awarding him $60,000 because the others had "negligently and intentionally committed adultery."

A fifty-six-year-old Indiana man registered for a motel room in Chattanooga, Tennessee. He picked up his room key, left the desk, and drove around to his room. Unlocking the door, he walked in and was stunned when confronted by a well-endowed "skimpily clad" female. In a state of shock, the fellow hurriedly exited the room. He brought suit against the motel, claiming that the desk clerk had given him the wrong room and that in "turning around and bolting out" of the room, he had suffered a ruptured disc. The court awarded him $25,000 plus medical costs.

So that's it! The world appears to be inundated with loony sex laws. Sex related legislation flows from the pens of lawmakers at every level of government. Hubert H. Humphrey was quite correct when he said: "There are not enough jails, not enough policemen, not enough courts to enforce a law not supported by the people." And this is probably even more true with the astounding number of laws designed to regulate sexuality. For as sex researcher William H. Masters so astutely observed: "If the sex laws were applied drastically, I wonder who the jailers would be."

Index